The 5-Minute Mindset

for Success Workbook

by Bob Hoffman

Published 2011 by Bob Hoffman, Sandy, Utah

Library of Congress Catalog Card #: 2011902620

ISBN: 978-0-9832412-2-5

Visit us at: www.The5-MinuteMindset.com

The 5-Minute Mindset

Taking just a few minutes a day to make sure you have the right mindset in place can make a huge difference in the quality of your life and the attitude with which you approach your opportunities or challenges.

Table of Contents

Introduction

Whether you want to make more money, start a business, become a more successful salesperson, improve your personal relationships, have a better marriage, lose weight or develop any successful habit or skill, **creating the right mindset will be the key to your success.**

A few years ago, I created a business that helped my sales associates accomplish some great things financially for themselves and their families. Schoolteachers, laborers and housewives working part time, made full time incomes that in some cases exceeded a six-figure income. Developing and maintaining the right mindset was the key to their success.

This system will work for any area of your life. For example: Recently, when I decided that weight loss was a priority in my life, I changed my mindset so powerfully that I took action and lost 73 pounds in five months.

By using this workbook, you will become familiar with the nine steps of the mindsetting process. As you apply these powerful mindsetting principles in your life, you will create and form new habits that promote happiness and success. You will learn how to overcome obstacles that in the past have kept you from achieving your goals and dreams.

Developing the right mindset may take some time initially, but once in place, it takes just minutes a day to maintain. **The 5-Minute Mindset** can and will change your life if you apply the nine steps of the process consistently.

You'll learn how to energize your decisions by **finding powerful 'whys', writing your own story, setting goals, staying motivated and making course corrections.** You'll also learn about staying ***'On It'*** and the importance of celebrating every success.

How many times have you heard someone say, "All you need to do is have the right mindset: Develop the right mindset and you'll be successful?" But that's as far as it goes. What is 'the right mindset' and how do you develop it? What does it mean? This workbook provides the answers to these questions and shows you how to develop and maintain **The 5-Minute Mindset**, which creates the right mindset you need for day-to-day successful living.

Every day we are faced with situations that require us to make choices and take action. When we take action with a successful mindset, we enhance our ability to succeed and achieve our goals and dreams.

The 5-Minute Mindset is not about developing just any mindset. It's about developing the right mindset you need for success and maintaining it.

"The 5-Minute Mindset for Success Workbook" is designed in such a way that it can be used for developing the right mindset for achieving any worthwhile goal or endeavor. Whether you want to create wealth, develop a healthier lifestyle, build stronger and happier relationships or develop a new skill or talent; developing the right mindset will be the most important thing you do.

The workbook includes examples that help you understand what the nine steps are and how to use them. The forms also give you a track to run on, a way to measure your progress.

After reading the outline of the steps, go to the **Forms Section** of the book. In this section you will find instructions and examples of **how to use and fill out the forms**. Behind the example section there are seven sets of personal forms for your use.

The 5-Minute Mindset

STEPS

Step 1
Make a Decision

Make a decision about what area in your life you want to improve. There are many areas of life for you to consider. Do you want to improve yourself financially, mentally, physically, socially or spiritually? You may want to earn more money, develop a healthier lifestyle, improve your family relationships, change your occupation or develop a new skill.

Maybe you want to be a better mother or father, a better spouse, a kinder person, healthier, a better employee, a more successful businessman, salesman, or student. Maybe you want to start a new business, find a more rewarding career, get a university education, or have more friends. **Improving in any of these areas requires that you develop the right mindset and developing the right mindset begins with a decision.**

Until you make a decision you will make little or no progress. What do you really want to accomplish? What are the real priorities of your life? You have to decide.

Your current actions speak volumes about the decisions you have made in the past. To get different results requires different actions and **different actions begin with a decision to change or improve something in your life.**

Don't try to change everything in your life at once. Narrow your choices down to two or three things. If this is your first experience using the **5-Minute Mindsetting** process, we suggest you choose just one area to start with. As you become more familiar with the mindsetting steps, add other areas as your time and skill allow.

While this first step sounds simple, it is one of the keys to your success. When you make a decision about an area on which to work and you are serious about it, your actions begin to change and you are on the road to developing new habits and creating the right mindset.

On page 32 and 33 you will find an example of the decision making process and the form that goes with it.

Step 2
Write Your Own Story and Find Your 'Whys'

Now that you have decided on an area to improve in your life, it's time to **write your own story and develop some powerful 'whys'.**

Writing your own story is about finding your **'whys'**-- the reasons you want to improve in that area. You can either make a list of your reasons or write about some of your life's experiences that made you realize how important it is for you to make a change.

Writing your own story or making a list of 'whys' strengthens your emotional attachment to your decision. Having a strong emotional attachment to your decision helps you overcome difficulties and solve problems when they arise.

Your stories and reasons clarify what you are trying to accomplish and encourage you to keep going and stay the course even when challenges come. Reviewing your 'whys' daily also strengthens your mindset helping you stick to the tasks at hand as you strive for success.

Asking yourself the right questions can help you create a list of powerful **'whys'**. Why did you choose a particular area to work on? Why is it so important to you? What are your personal reasons for the area in your life you want to improve? Why do you want to make more money? Why do you want to be a better friend; a better spouse? Why do you want have a healthier lifestyle? What are your reasons for losing weight? Why do you want to change your field of study or work? Why do you want to learn a new skill? Why do you want to be a better parent? Why do you want to be more successful in business? Why to you want to improve your sales skills? What experiences led to your current decision? How will the changes you envision affect your future?

Perhaps your most powerful **'whys'** will be in the form of **personal stories, observations, or experiences.** Writing these stories down can be a very important part of the mindsetting process.

For example: As I began to brainstorm and think about all the reasons I did not want to be overweight, I wrote these down in story form. These stories are available in my book **"The 5-Minute Mindset for Weight Loss."** As I went through this part of the mindsetting process, the commitment to develop a weight loss plan became an absolute commitment. My desire to lose weight and live healthier became so strong that I began to overcome the habits that kept me from losing weight. You have to have strong personal reasons for making a change before you can complete the mindsetting process.

Writing my own story helped me remember why I wanted to lose weight and stay the course when I felt like giving up or got discouraged.

We suggest that you come up with at least four or five reasons why you want to improve in your chosen area. Explain in detail why this area is so important to you and how making this change will affect your life and the lives of those you love.

Here are a few reasons I wanted to lose weight. I wanted to shop at regular stores and save money. I wanted to feel more comfortable in social settings, like eating out, going to movies or family gatherings. I wanted to have more energy for work and recreation. These are things I felt very deeply about. They provided me with the motivation I needed when I was faced with challenges or felt like giving up.

Most of my **'whys'** were written in the form of a story. Writing my stories was more powerful to me than just stating the reasons. How you choose to do this step is a personal choice. You can write personal stories or simply make a list, as long as they are meaningful and important to you. **The more personal and emotionally powerful you make your stories and your 'whys' the better your chances will be for developing the right mindset and achieving the related goals.**

Refer back to this step and add to your reasons throughout the mind setting process.

Losing 73 pounds in five months took a powerful mindset and writing my own story was a key component of that success. I spent a lot of time on this step in preparation for achieving my weight loss goals. I would frequently review my stories as part of my weight loss plan. Doing this helped me stay motivated and provided me with the reasons for staying with my plan and achieving my weight loss goals.

Spend enough time in writing your own story to **form strong personal reasons for improving.** Again, this may take a few minutes or it may take a few days. Make sure to write your story down in your workbook. Once you have written your story or found your reasons, spend some time every day reviewing them.

Remember, the more heartfelt and personal your stories and reasons are, the more determined you will be to accomplish whatever it is you have decided to do.

For an example of how to write your own story, find your 'whys' and use the related forms, go to pages 34 and 35 of the example section.

Step 3
Set Your Goals

Setting specific achievable goals with a deadline has a powerful effect on your mindset and writing them down increases that power. It sets the mind in motion looking for solutions of how to achieve your objectives and helps you begin to formulate a plan that will lead to success.

For example: After I decided to lose weight and wrote down some powerful personal reasons for doing so, I then set a long-term goal; **I am going to lose 120 pounds in 12 months.** Then I created an intermediate goal. I am going to lose 60 pounds in the next six months. I broke this goal down into a goal of losing 10 pounds per month. As I thought about my goals, I began to formulate ideas on how to achieve them.

When you set your goals, write them down in the workbook and plan on reviewing them daily. Make sure that your goals are specific and achievable. Depending on the goal, break it down into yearly, monthly, weekly, and daily goals. As you set your goals make the decision to never give in to setbacks, discouragement or a change in circumstance. Never quit and never give up!

Go into detail on this step and write down your specific achievable goals in the workbook. Have both short and long-term goals. Where do you want to be five years from now; one year from now; a month from now; a week from now; tomorrow?

Be reasonable in your thinking. Make your goals incremental and suited to your abilities. You will find it better if you write your goals down.

As you take action on your goals, other ideas and solutions to your unique challenges will surface. You don't necessarily have to wait until your goals are completely written down in every detail before you begin to take action on your goals.

Take a few minutes every day to measure and account for your goals. The workbook provides you with a simple form to help you do this. Good things happen when you account for your achievements for the day, week or month.

Stay focused on achieving your goals. Why are they important to you? How will it feel as you achieve them and make the wanted changes in your life? Keep your goals simple.

As you take just a few minutes a day to review your goals and account for them, you will get amazing results. Remember to see the big picture and realize that daily battles won or lost, may or may not win the war. Keep trying in spite of setbacks. You cannot fail unless you quit trying.

As you take action on your goals, your mindset will get stronger and carry you through difficult moments when you are tempted to veer off your chosen path. All of us have set goals and failed again and again. For some, setting goals has become a trite phrase with little meaning. **The mindsetting process is unique and dynamic, strengthening your resolve and commitment to achieving your long-term goals.**

With the right mind set in place, you make an absolute commitment to do whatever it takes to reach the destination in mind. **With the right mindset about your goals there can be no failure, only success.** You might lose a battle here and there but you choose not to give up, you choose to keep going and win the war. Every day you are closer to the dream and the vision you want to achieve.

As you make an absolute commitment to achieve your goals, the necessary resources begin to surface. You may also find others who have similar goals and will be interested in working with you.

Throughout history, there are examples of men and women who set goals and achieved them through a powerful mindset. One of these was Cortez. Cortez, upon landing in the new world was confronted by a nation of hundreds of thousands of natives; many were fierce and cunning warriors. When confronted by the challenge to conquer the land, some of his men wanted to return home to Spain. Cortez made the decision to stay and conquer the land for Spain. He burned his own ships that lay in the bay waiting to take them home and to safety. With a few cannons, some horses, and circumstances that played into the Spaniards' hands, they conquered the Aztecs and won glory for the Spanish crown. The course of history in the Americas was changed forever.

American History is filled with examples of men and women who achieved success through a powerful mindset. You might read some of their stories as an aid in helping you develop and strengthen yours.

You probably know stories of other men and women whose visions and dreams came to fruition because of determination, work and faith. There is no reason why you can't write a story of your own, a story of determination, courage and hope. **Setting goals is a key to this process after establishing powerful 'whys'.**

I'm sure that men like Columbus, Cortez, George Washington, and Abraham Lincoln had powerful 'whys' in place as they worked to achieve their goals for themselves and their countries.

The challenges we face in our own personal lives may not be as dramatic or great as the men mentioned, but the future of our lives and the lives of those we love will be impacted by the choices we make today and how we choose to face our difficulties and challenges. Developing a powerful mindset may determine if we are successful or not.

Every day I took a few minutes and fed my mind with ideas and thoughts about my weight loss goals. By feeding my mind with thoughts and ideas every day about my goals, I was able to strengthen my mindset and generate daily, weekly and monthly strategies which enabled me to form new habits and change the way I ate and exercised. You can do the same for whatever your goals may be.

Write down what you want to do specifically. Be sure that your goals are measurable and achievable. Set deadlines. Set daily, weekly, monthly and yearly goals. You may also set longer-term goals as well. Make a commitment to review your goals daily. Use the forms to set and account for your goals.

For an example of how to set goals and use the related forms go to pages 36 and 37 of the example section.

Step 4
Design a Plan

After setting your goals, you are ready to design a plan for achieving them. Your plan is the step-by-step process of how you will achieve your goals. Designing your plan strengthens and solidifies your mindset, increasing your chances for success.

Your plan consists of a set of tasks and actions that must be done if you are going to be successful. Your goals and plans form a map that will guide you to your desired results.

Would you start a vacation without thinking about the type of transportation you were going to use, how much time it will take, what tourist attractions you want to see or how much will it cost?

Would you start a business without a solid business plan? What is the purpose of your business? What benefits will your business provide for customers? What are the overhead costs that will need to be covered? How much start-up capital is needed?

Spending quality time designing a plan and preparing for success will pay big dividends.

As you design your plan, you will find that there are certain **core principles** that are essential to the achievement of your particular goal. For example, when I chose weight loss as my goal, I kept three **core principles** in mind; **develop a powerful mindset, eat healthier and be more active.** These became the core of my plan.

What are the core principles you need to work on for achieving your goals? Every area has core principles that form the foundation of your plan. The most important and perhaps vital of these is **developing the right mindset**.

I began my most recent weight loss effort by developing a powerful mindset. Going through this process was the single most important thing that I did and has been the key to long-term success.

Your mindset develops as you implement the steps and principles discussed in this book. Your plan should consist of reviewing your story, your goals, and the actions you must take to achieve your goals. Creating a workable plan is a process and takes time. How long, is up to you.

Sometimes you'll learn something new about your goal and decide to incorporate it into your plan immediately. You should always ask yourself how this idea fits into your plan and how it helps you achieve your main goal. Be sure to make note of these ideas as they come to mind. This list may become part of your plan. You may begin implementing these ideas immediately if you choose.

For example, as part of my weight loss plan, I decided to cut down on my fat gram intake. I did this by paying attention to the fat content of the foods I ate. I immediately implemented this plan and saw results.

My weight loss plan consists of a few basic rules that I review and do every day. This plan evolved over time. I didn't wait until a full plan was in writing. I had to change and adapt the plan to my circumstances. Over time, a working plan developed. Part of this plan is outlined for you in our example section of the workbook and should help you design your plan for whatever your goal(s) may be.

As you develop your strategies, implement them as you go. The sooner you begin getting results and achieving your goals, the stronger your mindset will become. Let your plan evolve as you take action.

As you design your plan, remember your reasons for achieving your goals. Review your 'whys.' Review your plans and goals daily. Doing this just a few minutes a day strengthens your mindset and reminds you of the strategies you will employ during the day in accomplishing your goals.

It's important to organize and prioritize your ideas and research into your own customized plan. **What are the core principles that form the foundation for your plan?** What hard and fast rules are you going to make for yourself that can facilitate your success? What steps do you need to take to achieve your goals? What strategies are you going to use?

By spending some time organizing your thoughts into a plan of action, you solidify your mindset and increase your chances for success.

Keep your plan simple and achievable.

For an example of how to design a plan and use the related forms, go to pages 38 and 39 of the example section.

Step 5
Implement the Plan

Implementing the plan means taking action. You have already taken action toward developing your **5-minute mindset** by purchasing this workbook, making a decision, writing your own story, setting your goals and designing a plan.

Now it's time to focus and fully implement your plan. Take action. Keep your commitments. Be *'On It!'*

Being 'On It' means that you are fully involved in achieving your plan on a daily, weekly and monthly basis. You are keeping your commitments according to your plan. Every day before you leave the house you think about and review your goals and plans. This process should take about five minutes. You make commitments and complete the plan for the day so at the end of the day you can say, "I did it; I kept my commitments." You want to do the same thing for the week. You can't be *'On It'* until you are fully engaged in completing the work as outlined in your plan.

Implementing your plan is like a plane taking off. When an aircraft takes off, there has to be a flight plan. There is a pilot and a co-pilot who checks each system to make sure the plane is ready to fly. Take-off is the most dangerous and difficult moment for pilots. The plane must achieve a certain speed before take-off. Gaining the momentum and speed necessary requires a lot of energy and fuel. Once the plane reaches cruising altitude, less energy is required to keep the plane aloft.

You have found the right runway; you're beginning to taxi. Now you have to apply enough energy to get the plane off the ground.

The energy you put into your previous steps is now ready to be released by steady and consistent action until you reach your cruising altitude. Achieving take-off and reaching your cruising altitude is being *'On it.'*

As you take off, there could be wind sheer or other dangerous conditions that may make the take off difficult. Through proper preparation, you are ready for whatever you need to do to get the plane up. This is also part of being *'On It.'*

A pilot has to be aware of the course, direction, and altitude of the plane. Air controllers help pilots maintain their flight plan and stay on course to their destination. Sometimes course corrections during the flight are necessary to bring the plane to its destination.

Maybe you have to change altitude or direction to get around or above a storm. Hopefully, you have enough fuel to meet the demands.

As you think about being *'On it'* and implementing your own plan, review your own story, keeping the plane analogy in mind.

Sometimes, finding a coach or a partner to work with can create synergism and excitement for the successful accomplishment of your goal.

It's good to have most of your plan in place, but don't wait too long before you begin to act. Maintaining the right mindset may very well depend on you beginning right away. You will gain confidence as you implement even part of your plan and begin to have some success. The sooner you begin having some success, the more likely you are to follow through with the rest of your plan.

You've designed a plan that identifies a few core principles related to your decision and goals. You've also identified some habits that you need to change that will help you achieve your goals. Now do them. What commitments are you going to make today to get the results you want?

You're already spending some time every day reviewing and thinking about your goals. Your plan for accomplishing your goals is taking shape. You have some ideas of what you want to do and you are ready to take steady and consistent action toward achieving your focused goals. As you take steady and consistent action, new skills and talents will begin to form. At times you may be tempted to drift from your plan because of illness or other circumstances. Remember your decisions; stay with it.

Implementing your plan, taking action and achieving your goals bring positive results. Positive results strengthen your mindset.

Your long-term success will be determined by focused daily activity.

As you take action by implementing your plan you begin to reap the benefits of having a powerful mindset. These benefits include more freedom, more self-respect, and more opportunity. Your desire for more success grows as you begin to see results. You become more committed to practicing the **5-Minute Mindset** daily.

Keep the implementation of your plan simple and achievable.

Use the weekly goal-planning sheet to track your progress and success.

For an example of how to implement a plan and use the related forms, go to page 42 and 43 of the example section.

Step 6
Provide Ongoing Motivation

As you implement your plan, obstacles and challenges will begin to surface. Daily motivation becomes critical to your success. What inspires you? Who inspires you? Do you know any inspirational quotes, stories, or sayings that will encourage you to stick with your plan and not give up?

We have provided a few inspirational thoughts and left several blank forms for your use as you find your own personal resources for motivation and inspiration.

Your own story acts as the **core motivation** for your program. It contains your **'motivational whys'** and should be reviewed often to avoid discouragement and setbacks. Using the inspirational thoughts and success stories of others can also help you stay motivated and on track. You should think about your own story and add to it often.

How do you stay motivated when you have a setback? How do you develop the courage to see beyond the challenge and see the success waiting for you just around the corner?

Setbacks occur when circumstances change and you don't achieve your weekly or monthly goals. How do you stay motivated and get back *'On it?'* Staying motivated when you get discouraged or experience a setback is very important to your ultimate success.

Realize that you cannot avoid setbacks; they will happen. However, you can choose how you will respond.

Remember the airplane analogy. It needs fuel to stay in the air and arrive at its destination. Motivation is the fuel that will get you in the air, keep you on your desired course, enable you to keep *'On It'*, and reach your destination, in spite of discouragement and setbacks. Making sure that an airplane has enough fuel is critical to a successful flight. Planning and having enough ongoing motivation is critical to achieving your goals and creating the right mindset.

I memorized the following poems and review them daily, especially when I'm tempted to stray from my goals or plan.

There can be no fullness of life where there is slavery.
The man who is subject to his appetite is the most abject slave.
The man who can rule his passions is greater than a king.
Author Unknown

Stick to your task, 'til it sticks to you
Beginners are many, Enders are few
Honor, power, peace, and praise
Will come in time to the one who stays.

Stick to your task, 'til it sticks to you
Bend at it, sweat at it, smile at it too
For out of the bend and the sweat and the smile
Will come life's victories after awhile.
Author Unknown

Here are a few other examples of other inspiring stories and quotes:

Sew a thought
Reap an act

Sew an act
Reap a habit

Sew a habit
Reap a character

Sew a character
Reap a destiny
Author Unknown

In World War Two, during the battle for England, when England for a time stood virtually alone against German aggression, Germany was pounding London with incessant bombing. There was the constant threat of invasion and many were killed. Winston Churchill inspired his people to continue resisting with these words: "We shall defend our island, whatever the cost may be, we shall fight on the beaches, we shall fight on the landing grounds, we shall fight in the fields and in the streets, we shall fight in the hills; we shall never surrender." His words and leadership inspired a nation to stay the course and not give up.

Were there setbacks? Did England lose some battles on the road to victory? Where would the world be today if England had given up and surrendered? Winston Churchill understood the importance of developing a successful mindset for himself and his people. He also said, "Success is going from failure to failure without a loss of enthusiasm." The key is never giving up or giving in.

In the early 1950's, Harland Sanders, known as Colonel Sanders, owned a gas station in Kentucky. He sold gas and served meals to hungry travelers. His meals included his celebrated chicken, made from a recipe that he had perfected over a twenty-year period. When a state highway was built that bypassed his store in Corbin, Kentucky, his business dried up and he was left only with his social security check as income. He decided to sell the rights to his chicken for a small piece of the profit on each sale. He travelled from one restaurant to another trying to convince them to pay him to use his recipe. He spoke to over 900 restaurant owners before meeting with Pete Harman, of Salt Lake City, who took the Colonel up on his offer. Pete Harman worked closely with the Colonel in developing the franchise until Colonel Sanders sold the franchise in 1964 for $2,000,000. He continued as a spokesman for the franchise until his death in 1980.

This quote sums up his life and philosophy: "I made a resolve then that I was going to amount to something if I could and no hours, no amount of labor, no amount of money would deter me from giving the best that there was in me. I have done that ever since, and I win by it. I know."

Ongoing motivation can be as simple as reviewing your own story, reminding yourself what you want to do and why, becoming familiar with the success stories of others, and memorizing a few simple poems. Mix and match these techniques as your circumstances and needs require.

If you choose, you can read the biographies of people who overcame incredible odds to become successful; they are all around us. Learn about some of the following people and how they became successful: Helen Keller, George Washington, Ben Franklin, Madame Curie, Thomas Edison, Mahatma Gandhi, Abraham Lincoln, Dwight Eisenhower or Mother Teresa. There are so many great stories about men and women who faced adversity and achieved their goals. Choose a few of their stories and learn about them. Use their stories and some of their quotes to stay motivated and keep on track.

If you spend time reading about the success of others, write summaries of what impressed you most about their courage, determination, hard work, and persistence that you can review and use for your own motivation.

Why not, in our own spheres, add our names to the list of great people. Not that we need to rise to obtain the world's recognition for our accomplishments, but simply that we have made our homes and communities better places to live. Can achieving your goals do this? I don't know, but you'll feel better, and you'll have more self-esteem. **Could you change the world? If you succeed, you've changed yours.**

Sharing your successful experiences and what you've learned with others is another way to find encouragement and support. One way to do this is to find a partner who has the same concerns and interests as you.

Remembering your successful experiences when the going gets tough or you have a setback can also provide much needed inspiration.

Summing It Up

Spend a few minutes each day remembering what you want to accomplish and why. Also review your plan for the day. Use the workbook to record and track your goals. Review inspirational poems and stories that inspire you and will help you stay *'On it.'* You may consider working together with someone who has similar aspirations and goals.

At the end of the day, think about the commitments and the goals you have achieved and feel good about them. Take a minute and note your success in your workbook.

For an example of how to provide ongoing motivation and use the related forms, go to pages 44 and 45 of the example section.

Step 7
Interpret Your Results and Adjust Accordingly

As you implement your plan, you will begin to have results. Are you achieving the results that you expected?

During a flight, a pilot continually checks his instruments, making sure the plane is still on course and moving toward its destination. Likewise, it's important for you to continue to review your goals and make sure you are achieving the results you want.

Interpreting your results means that on a regular basis (daily or weekly), you are evaluating your progress to determine if a course correction is needed.

In this phase of developing a successful mindset, your plan is fully implemented and you're beginning to see results. You feel good about what you're accomplishing, but you've experienced some minor setbacks or you foresee some challenges ahead that will distract you from working on your goals and implementing your plans. Maybe you become ill; a vacation is coming up; a serious family issue arises. Don't worry. By doing the **5-Minute Mindsetting** steps daily, even if you experience a setback, you'll be prepared for most challenges and will be able to get back *'On it.'* This is the key. You can only fail if you don't get back *'On it.'*

Don't be afraid to adjust your goals or plan in order to get the results you want. Courage, determination and persistence will win the day. Try again tomorrow.

You will find that as you begin to implement your plan, things happen. Life puts up obstacles that make writing your new story challenging and difficult: The price of success is higher than anticipated. Someone you admire criticizes your efforts. You become ill or your employment changes. Whatever it is, life happens and circumstances change.

When I first set my weight loss goals, I really didn't think about how I would feel when Thanksgiving and Christmas rolled around. Like most families, eating is a big event around Thanksgiving and this particular year we were planning to be in Hawaii over the Christmas holiday. I had already lost a lot of weight by Thanksgiving. I could easily have chosen to allow myself some slack. Instead, I chose to stick with my plan and eat within my chosen healthy food groups. Although I allowed myself to eat a little more over Thanksgiving and Christmas, I still continued to lose weight. I was *'On it.'*

If you see that a course adjustment is needed, don't try to change too many habits at once. Developing the **5-Minute Mindset** is a process. You will learn as you go. Continue down the path and you will find the resources and help you need as you meet new and challenging situations.

Deciding when and what course corrections are needed require the ability to evaluate your progress. As you decide on needed course corrections, asking yourself the right questions is very important. Here are a few examples: Why am I not achieving this daily goal? What am I doing that is making it difficult for me to focus? What do I need to do to stay motivated? Am I doing everything I can to achieve my weekly and monthly goals? Do I have the right mindset?

As you evaluate your progress, you may find ways to improve your plan or recognize the need to adjust your goals.

After implementing my weight loss plan, I began losing weight too fast. By too fast, I mean 4 to 5 lbs in two to three days. Research indicates losing weight that fast is unhealthy. I wanted to lose weight at a nice steady pace and keep the weight off for good. So, I adjusted my eating in such a way as to slow down the weight loss to a healthier pace. I kept eating plenty of low fat foods, fruits and vegetables, but I ate more of them. I would also allow myself to eat low fat sweets such as low fat cookies, candy and ice cream. There are a number of companies that make good tasting low fat ice cream, cookies, candy and other products.

After my weight was about the same for a period of time, I would go back to eating smaller portions. In this way I maintained a healthy weight loss rate. It took a while before I started getting the results I wanted, losing 2-3 pounds per week.

Having the proper mindset in place from the beginning was critical for me as I evaluated my progress. I made decisions about how much weight to lose in a month and how I was going to eat during a vacation or other event.

Regardless of your goal, even with the right mindset, you will have unexpected challenges to face. I was involved in a car accident that resulted in some back and neck issues for me. My weight loss program suddenly needed help. I couldn't exercise as much and was in pain all the time. I wanted to eat more. Most of you know what it is like when you don't feel well. In spite of this setback, I was able to keep off most of the weight that I had lost. My mindset and new set of eating habits made this possible. I reviewed my story, my plan and motivations. This encouraged me not to give up but stick with it. As I began to improve, I was able to get back on track with my weight loss program and began losing weight again.

If you have an unexpected circumstance in your life that takes you off your plan for a time, just remember you can get back *'On It'* quickly by repeating steps 1-9.

You've already done the steps once; they should fall into place for you faster the next time. Review your story and remind yourself about what you are doing and why.

Review your inspirational thoughts or memorize a new one. Maybe stronger motives are needed. Maybe your goals are too aggressive. Set new monthly goals. Evaluate your plan and decide what needs to be adjusted, if anything. When something unexpected happens, feel free to adjust your plans and your goals, but keep the ultimate destination in mind. During this evaluation process, you'll get ideas of what you need to change in order to accomplish your goals. Don't quit! Today is a new day and success is just around the corner.

You may feel that you do not have control of your own destiny, but you do. You decide what you think about. You decide how you will respond to any challenge.

If you experience a setback, re-read your story or list of 'whys' in your workbook. Look at the resources you have that might help. As you review your successes and failures, focus on the successes and re-commit to the habits that brought you success.

Recommitting to successful habits will lead to more success. Decide to stay with your overall plan and don't quit. During a course adjustment, if you get discouraged write about what is going on in your workbook and decide on what you are going to do to improve. **Remember the core principles and make adjustments. Do what you have to do to get the results that you want.** Keep it simple and stay with it!!! You can do it!

You will find that during your success journey, you will need to make occasional course adjustments. Keeping and maintaining the right mindset will insure that you do not stray too far from the main goal.

At one point in time, I wasn't losing the weight that I wanted to. After reviewing the mind setting process, I realized that I needed to change my bad eating habits; exercise simply wasn't enough. This was a major course correction for me. I re-did my eating plan and committed to the change. This helped me keep my commitments through Thanksgiving and Christmas and lose 73 pounds in the process.

You have to know what your results are before you can make adjustments. Part of my weight loss plan includes weighing myself Monday through Saturday at the gym. Some days my weight goes up a pound then it drops two. Keeping track of my success and failures from week to week helps me make course adjustments to my mindset, eating, and exercise habits.

The daily/weekly goal forms for step 4 and 5 help you evaluate your progress as you work on your goals.

In Summary

Spend a few minutes every day reviewing what you want to do and why. Think about your goals for the day using your workbook as a guide.

What are you going to do to be *'On It'* today?

Make course adjustments, if needed, to better fit your circumstances. Never lose sight of your overall goals. Stay motivated by reading stories of successful people or reading other success literature. You can stay motivated by reviewing your story and remembering how important your goals are to you. Or if you are struggling with motivation, talk with a friend.

The more involved you become in the **5-Minute Mindsetting** process, the better you will understand it and the more success you will have. If you aren't seeing the success you want, then check each of the steps and ask yourself how you can engage in these steps more proactively?

For an example of how to interpret your results, adjust your plan, and use the related forms, go to pages 44 and 45 of the example section.

Step 8
Celebrate Your Success

Celebrating your success along the way is an important feature of the **5-Minute Mindsetting** process. During each phase it's important to celebrate your successes, no matter how small they may be. When you complete that first daily goal or task, celebrate it. The sooner you begin to have some success and celebrate it, the more likely you are to go on and complete the next steps of the process.

You should plan ways to celebrate your successes. Celebrating a success can be as simple as checking off your achievement in your workbook, or after achieving a major goal, rewarding yourself in a way that's meaningful to you.

Part of celebrating your success is sharing what you've learned and accomplished with others.

Nothing is more satisfying than seeing a friend or an acquaintance pick up a few ideas that can make a difference in their lives and see them succeed. Supporting others in developing the right mindset and achieving their goals and dreams helps strengthen yours .

Watching my brother and others apply the principles in this book and seeing the great results they are having is very rewarding.

Celebrating every success as part of your **5-Minute Mindsetting** journey further strengthens your mindset.

For an example of how to celebrate your success and use the related forms go to page 46 and 47 of the example section.

Step 9
Arrive at Your Destination

As a plane comes in for a landing, the pilot checks the landing gear and other systems to make sure all is ready for landing. Landing is another dangerous phase for pilots. Anything can happen and different circumstances can make the landing very dangerous. If you are well prepared and trained, landing can be the best part of any flight.

After achieving your major goal, spend some time and enjoy it before going on to another area in your life to work on. Maintain the right mindset about the changes you've made in your life if you wish to keep and maintain the benefits that you are now reaping.

Congratulations, you have achieved your goal. You have stayed motivated and are excited to move on to other goals. Be careful. Don't forget what you have learned about achieving this goal and why it was important to you.

Remember how much you've changed and enjoy it. You've gained self-esteem, inner strength and formed new habits. You are greater than a king or queen.

By spending just five minutes a day, you can maintain a powerful mindset. By reviewing your 'whys', goals and plans just a few minutes a day, you'll keep the successful skills and habits in place.

Remember to keep your new mindset intact.

You may choose to work on other areas of your life and develop new talents and skills using the **5-Minute Mindsetting** process.

For an example of how to use the related forms for arriving at your destination go to page 46 and 47 of the example section.

The 5-Minute Mindset

EXAMPLE SECTION

The Example section provides the following:

1. A review of each mindsetting step and instructions on how to use the associated form are on the left.

2. On the right hand side is an example of how the form is used.

3. At the end of the **Example Section** is the **Forms Section**. The Forms Section contains seven complete sets of forms for steps 1-9 of the mindsetting process.

Step 1
Make a Decision

Using this form will help you make decisions about what area in your life you want to work on.

There are many areas for you to consider. Do you want to improve financially, mentally, physically, socially or spiritually? What are you passionate about? Use this form to brainstorm and write down any ideas that you have.

After brainstorming, prioritize your ideas by assigning them a number based on what is most important to you.

We recommend beginning with just one area to work on while you are learning the system. Add other areas as you choose.

5-Minute Mindset — Step 1: Make A Decision

What area do you want to work on?
(Example: Spiritual, Physical, Social, Emotional, Educational, Financial)

4	Pay off the house
3	Lose 50 pounds
2	Make $100,000 over the next 12 months
1	Improve my relationship with my spouse
5	Learn a foreign language
6	Earn a Master's or Doctorate degree in engineering
8	Become a successful business owner
7	Read 10 books in the next 12 months

Step 2
Write Your Own Story and Find Your 'Whys'

Now that you have decided on an area in your life to improve, it's time to **support your decision with some powerful 'whys'**. Perhaps one of the most important ways to do this is to write your own story. Writing your own story is about finding your **'whys'** in the experiences and observations of your daily life -- the reasons you want to improve in that area and writing them down. What experiences support your decision? Why did you choose a particular area to work on? Why is it so important to you?

Rather than writing your own story, you might prefer to make a list of reasons that support your decision. What are your personal reasons for the area in your life you want to improve?

Why do you want to make more money? Why do you want to be a better friend, a better spouse? Why do you want have a healthier lifestyle? What are your reasons for losing weight? Why do you want to change your field of study or work? Why do you want to learn a new skill? Why do you want to be a better parent? How will you and your family benefit from this decision? How will others benefit?

Be realistic about who you are and what you want to change. Write about whatever will motivate you to succeed, either positive or negative.

Use the Step 2 form to write your own story or make a list of your **'whys.'**

The 5-Minute Mindset

Step 2: Write Your Story and Find Your 'Whys'

What area in your life did you decide to work on?

I am extremely overweight, and I want to lose 50 pounds

Make a list of your reasons for this decision or write stories that illustrate why this decision is important to you.

Sample List of 'Whys':

When I go shopping, its embarrassing to have a cart full of junk food.

Shopping for clothes would be a lot funner.

Family activities would be more enjoyable.

I'll feel better about myself; more self esteem and more energy.

Sample Story:

As a young man about the age of 14, I went water skiing for the first time at a wonderful lake called

Lake Powell. I can remember laying there in the water, yelling at Bruce, the driver, to hit it and up

I came! Yep. First time up and away I went. I certainly thought that I was a hot shot to be

able to get up and ski my very first try.

Now, years later, getting up to ski has become increasingly difficult. However, even with the added

weight, I have always been able to get up and do a little skiing. Sometimes it has taken a try

or two to get up, but hey, what do you expect with a little extra weight and a few extra years?

However, for a person with an ego the size of mine, the unthinkable in fact happened; I could

not get up. As impossible as it seemed, disaster finally struck. I was so fat I could not get

up and ski. My wife and kids had never seen this before. But, true story, I could not get up.

Step 3
Set Your Goals

Now it's time to begin setting specific goals.

For example: After I decided to lose weight and wrote down some powerful personal reasons for doing so, I then set a long-term goal; **I am going to lose 120 pounds in 12 months.** Then I created intermediate goals; I am going to lose 60 pounds in the next six months. This I broke down into a goal of losing 10 pounds per month.

Make sure that your goals are specific and achievable. Break the goal down into long-term and intermediate goals. Long-term goals may be as long as 20 years or as short as a month. Intermediate goals can be yearly, monthly, or weekly depending on the goal. Short-term goals are usually weekly and daily goals. The Step 3 form is for long-term and intermediate goals. The Step 4 forms are for working with and tracking weekly and daily goals.

Go into detail on this step and write down your specific achievable goals. Make your goals incremental and suited to your abilities.

Take a few minutes every day to measure and account for your goals. Use the form provided to help you do this.

Use the example as a guide for setting your goals and accounting for your success.

One of the exciting features of the Step 3 goal setting form is the **achievement bar**. This bar helps you measure your success as you progress toward success with any given goal. After a deadline for a goal comes, fill in the percentage of your success on the achievement bar with a marker, pen, or pencil. You have an achievement bar for your main goal and intermediate goals.

Your daily and weekly goals can be set and tracked using the Step 4 Daily/Weekly Goal Tracker form.

The 5-Minute Mindset

Step 3: Set Goals
Long Term and Intermediate

Long Term Goal: Lose 120 lbs	Deadline	Goal	Actual
	1 yr	lose 120	

Achievement Bar

	25%	50%	75%	100%

Intermediate Goals or Tasks	Deadline	Goal	Actual	Achievement Bar
Lose 10 lbs	1-Mar	10	5	25 50 75 100
Lose 10 lbs	1-Apr	10	7	25 50 75 100
Lose 10 lbs	1-May	10	8	25 50 75 100
Lose 10 lbs	1-Jun	10	10	25 50 75 100
Lose 10 lbs	1-Jul	10	5	25 50 75 100
Lose 10 lbs	1-Aug	10	6	25 50 75 100
Lose 10 lbs	1-Sep	10	9	25 50 75 100
				25 50 75 100
				25 50 75 100
				25 50 75 100
				25 50 75 100
				25 50 75 100
				25 50 75 100
				25 50 75 100
				25 50 75 100
				25 50 75 100
				25 50 75 100

Step 4
Design a Plan

After setting your goals, you are ready to design a plan for achieving them. Your plan is a step-by-step process that consists of a set of tasks and actions as well as rules and guidelines that will help you achieve your goals. These should be focused around a set of core principles.

There are two forms used for **Step 4.**

1. Brainstorm; Resources, Principles, Rules, and Guidelines.
2. Daily/Weekly Goal Tracker

Use the Brainstorming section to make a rough draft of ideas, tasks and actions that will assist you in achieving your goal. **Seek for the core principles that will be the keys to your success.** Once you find the core principles associated with your goal, keep them in mind as you design your plan.

Prioritize your ideas and put the ones you want to track into the Daily/Weekly Goal Tracker. We will discuss the second form on page 40.

5-Minute Mindset
The

Step 4: Design a Plan
Brainstorm; Resources,
Principles, Rules and Guidelines

Goal / Due Date:

What resources of information are available to you? Do you know any experts? What are the hard and fast rules that will lead to success? What are the core principles? What guidelines are you going to set? How are you going to achieve your goal?

Priority	Entries
1	Drink more water
2	Watch the fat content of the foods I eat
3	Walk 40 minutes a day
4	Buy a treadmill
5	Join a local health club
6	I know a friend who has recently lost a lot of weight. How did she do it?
	Core Principles:
	Develop the right mindset
	Eat right
	Exercise

Step 4
Design a Plan (Continued)

After prioritizing your ideas, put the ones you want to track into the Daily/Weekly Goal Tracker. By reviewing your plan you will find some of your activities can be set up as goals and tasks. You don't need to track your entire plan. Some parts of your plan may only need to be reviewed occasionally in order to maintain the right mindset.

Write your main goal by the GOALS section on the form. Write the specific task in the 'Daily/Weekly Task' section of the form. If the goal applies to a particular day, place an 'x' in the 'goal' section of the form.

The goal may be a number. Instead of placing an 'x' in the goal section place the number that you want to achieve. (See example)

5-Minute Mindset

Step 4: Design a Plan
Step 5: Implement a Plan

Month___July_____

Daily/Weekly Goal Tracker

GOAL(S)　Lose 120 pounds by the end of this year

Daily/Weekly Tasks	Date	Mon 9	Tue 10	Wed 11	Thur 12	Fri 13	Sat 14	Sun 15	Total	Achievement Bar
Drink more water	Goal	✖	✖	✖	✖	✖	✖	✖	7	25 50 75 100
	Actual									
Walk 40 minutes / day	Goal	40		40		40			120	25 50 75 100
	Actual									
Eat less than 12 grams of fat / day	Goal	✖	✖	✖	✖	✖	✖	✖	7	25 50 75 100
	Actual									
Lose 4 pounds this week	Goal	205		Weight goal 201 lbs				201	4 lbs	25 50 75 100
	Actual	205								
	Goal									25 50 75 100
	Actual									

Daily/Weekly Tasks	Date	Mon	Tue	Wed	Thur	Fri	Sat	Sun	Total	Achievement Bar
	Goal									25 50 75 100
	Actual									
	Goal									25 50 75 100
	Actual									
	Goal									25 50 75 100
	Actual									
	Goal									25 50 75 100
	Actual									
	Goal									25 50 75 100
	Actual									

Daily/Weekly Tasks	Date	Mon	Tue	Wed	Thur	Fri	Sat	Sun	Total	Achievement Bar
	Goal									25 50 75 100
	Actual									
	Goal									25 50 75 100
	Actual									
	Goal									25 50 75 100
	Actual									
	Goal									25 50 75 100
	Actual									
	Goal									25 50 75 100
	Actual									

Step 5
Implement the Plan

You've completed the first four steps of the mindsetting process. Now the fun begins! Go to work and enjoy your success.

An important part of implementing your plan is tracking your progress.

You have placed an ' x' for which goals apply for a day. If you achieve the goal for that day place a check in the 'Actual' section of the form. If you don't achieve the goal for the day, mark it with a zero in the 'Actual' section of the form.

For setting and tracking goals involving numbers, place the number in the 'Goal' section of the form under the appropriate day. Place the actual number achieved in the 'Actual' section of the form. Both the 'Goal' numbers and the 'Actual' numbers can be totaled for the week.

Dividing the 'Actual' total by the 'Goal' total gives you the percentage of goal achieved for the 'Achievement Bar.'

Now it's time to focus and fully implement your plan. Take action. Keep your commitments. Be *'On It.'* Being *'On It'* means that you are fully involved in achieving your plan on a daily, weekly, and monthly basis. You are keeping your commitments according to your plan. Every day before you leave the house you think about and review your goals and plan. This process should take about five minutes. You make commitments and complete the plan for the day so at the end of the day you can say, "I did it; I kept my commitments." You want to do the same thing for the week.

As you do this you will find your days and weeks becoming more productive and fruitful. Your days will be filled with opportunities to stick to your go goals and tasks. At the end of the day you can take satisfaction in all that you've accomplished. Reviewing your goals briefly every day will bring great results.

The Step 4 and 5 form is designed in such a way that you can create daily and weekly goals and keep track of your progress on the same form.

You can't be *'On It'* until you are fully engaged in completing the work as outlined in your plan and tracking it in the Daily/Weekly Goal Tracker.

The 5-Minute Mindset

Step 4: Design a Plan
Step 5: Implement a Plan
Daily/Weekly Goal Tracker

Month July

GOAL(S) Lose 120 pounds by the end of this year

Daily/Weekly Tasks		Mon	Tue	Wed	Thur	Fri	Sat	Sun	Total	Achievement Bar
	Date	9	10	11	12	13	14	15		
Drink more water	Goal	✖	✖	✖	✖	✖	✖	✖	7	25 50 75 100
	Actual	✔	✔	0	✔	✔	0	✔	5	�
Walk 40 minutes / day	Goal	40		40		40			120	25 50 75 100
	Actual	40		40		40			120	██████
Eat less than 12 grams of fat / day	Goal	✖	✖	✖	✖	✖	✖	✖	7	25 50 75 100
	Actual	✔	✔	0	✔	0	✔	0	4	▒▒
Lose 4 pounds this week	Goal	205		Weight goal	201 lbs			201	4 lbs	25 50 75 100
	Actual	205	204	204	205	204	203	203	2 lbs	▒
	Goal									25 50 75 100
	Actual									

Daily/Weekly Tasks		Mon	Tue	Wed	Thur	Fri	Sat	Sun	Total	Achievement Bar
	Date									
	Goal									25 50 75 100
	Actual									
	Goal									25 50 75 100
	Actual									
	Goal									25 50 75 100
	Actual									
	Goal									25 50 75 100
	Actual									
	Goal									25 50 75 100
	Actual									

Daily/Weekly Tasks		Mon	Tue	Wed	Thur	Fri	Sat	Sun	Total	Achievement Bar
	Date									
	Goal									25 50 75 100
	Actual									
	Goal									25 50 75 100
	Actual									
	Goal									25 50 75 100
	Actual									
	Goal									25 50 75 100
	Actual									
	Goal									25 50 75 100
	Actual									

Step 6
Provide Ongoing Motivation

As you implement your plan, obstacles and challenges will begin to surface. Daily motivation becomes critical to your success. What inspires you? Who inspires you? Do you know any inspirational quotes, stories or sayings that will encourage you to stick with your plan and not give up?

As you find your personal sources of inspiration use the journal pages provided.

Step 7
Interpret Your Results and Adjust Accordingly

As you implement your plan you will begin to have results. Are you achieving the results that you expected?

Interpreting your results means that on a regular basis (daily or weekly), you are evaluating your progress to determine if a course correction is needed. The **'achievement bars'** are one way to measure your results. You can also use the forms provided as a journal of events and how you are doing with your goals.

You will find that as you begin to implement your plan, things happen. Life puts up obstacles that will make writing your new story challenging and difficult: The price of success is higher than anticipated. Someone you admire criticizes your efforts. You become ill or your employment changes. Whatever it is, life happens and circumstances change.

By doing the **5-Minute Mindsetting** steps daily, even if you experience a minor or major setback, you'll be prepared for most challenges and will be able to get back *'On it.'* This is the key. You can only fail if you don't get back *'On it.'* Always plan to get back to your plan and goals.

Don't be afraid to adjust your goals or plan in order to get the results you want. Use the forms provided to make note of these ideas and adjustments as needed, then revise your plans and goals. Don't give up on your main goal. Remember that courage, determination, and persistence will win the day. Try again tomorrow.

5-Minute Mindset	**Step 6: Provide Ongoing Motivation** **Step 7: Interpret Results and Adjust Accordingly** **Step 8: Celebrate Your Success** **Step 9: Arrive at Your Destination**
Date	**Entries**
6/9	I looked at myself in the mirror today. I am sick of being so fat. Today I am going to eat right drink plent of water and exercise.
6/15	I recently learned that overweight people have a higher probability of developing diabetes. I don't want to be in that position.
6/30	Memorized a poem today called 'Sow a Thought'. I'm going to think about this today.
8/15	One of my good friends noticed that I have been losing weight. It made me feel good that others are beginning to notice my improvement.
9/25	I can do a little better being *'On It.'* This week my mindset wasn't as strong as it has been. I am going to do better today.

Step 8
Celebrate Your Success

Celebrating your success along the way is an important feature of the **5-Minute Mindsetting** process. During each phase, it's important to celebrate your successes, no matter how small they may be. When you complete that first daily goal or task, celebrate it. The sooner you begin to have some success and celebrate it, the more likely you are to go on and complete the next step of the process.

Use the journal pages and make a list of how you'd like to celebrate the achievement of your goals or write how you feel about your successes. How you celebrate is up to you. Sharing your success with others is another way of celebrating your success.

Celebrating your successes will strengthen your mindset, helping you look past the challenges and obstacles that may occur.

Step 9
Arrive at Your Destination

After achieving your goal, you may choose to use some journal pages and make note of the date the goal was accomplished, how you celebrated and how your life has changed as a result of your hard work and effort.

You've gained self-esteem, inner strength and formed new habits. Make note of some of the habits and what is different about your life.

Remember that spending just five minutes a day, will maintain a powerful mindset. By reviewing your 'whys,' goals and plans just a few minutes a day, you'll keep the successful skills and habits in place.

As you choose other areas in your life to change, repeat the **5-Minute Mindsetting proess.**

5-Minute Mindset	**Step 6: Provide Ongoing Motivation** **Step 7: Interpret Results and Adjust Accordingly** **Step 8: Celebrate Your Success** **Step 9: Arrive at Your Destination**
Date	**Entries**
7/1	Reached weekly goal. Went shopping had a great time.
7/25	This month I made some great progress. I've already lost 8 pounds.
8/1	Exercised according to plan. I feel great.
8/3	Shared the 5-Minute Mindset with 4 friends. They have all bought the book and are beginning to make great progress.
8/15	One of my good friends noticed that I have been losing weight.
8/25	Everyone is noticing the weight I've lost. This is so cool!!!
9/20	Making plans for a trip to the Bahamas as soon as I reach my goal. Almost there.

The 5-Minute Mindset

FORMS SECTION

Use this form to track your mindsetting progress in
each area you are working on.

What area(s) are you working on?

The 5-Minute Mindset Tracker

Steps	Form for #	1	2	3	4	5	6	7
	Page #	51	79	107	135	163	191	219
1. Make a Decision								
2. What are Your 'Whys'								
3. Set Goals								
4. Design a Plan								
5. Implement the Plan								
6. Stay Motivated								
7. Interpret Your Results								
8. Celebrate Every Success								
9. Arrive at Your Destination								

The 5-Minute Mindset

Forms for # 1

**(After you decide what area you want to work
on, come back to this page and fill it in.)**

_____

_____

_____

The 5-Minute Mindset	**Step 1: Make A Decision**
	What area do you want to work on? (Example: Spiritual, Physical, Social, Emotional, Educational, Financial)

5-Minute Mindset

Step 2: Write Your Story and Find Your 'Whys'

What area in your life did you decide to work on?

Make a list of your reasons for this decision or write stories that illustrate why this decision is important to you.

5-Minute Mindset

Step 2: Write Your Story and Find Your 'Whys'

What area in your life did you decide to work on?

Make a list of your reasons for this decision or write stories that illustrate why this decision is important to you.

The 5-Minute Mindset

Step 3: Set Goals
Long Term and Intermediate

Long Term Goal:	Deadline	Goal	Actual

Achievement Bar

25%	50%	75%	100%

Intermediate Goals or Tasks	Deadline	Goal	Actual	Achievement Bar
				25 50 75 100
				25 50 75 100
				25 50 75 100
				25 50 75 100
				25 50 75 100
				25 50 75 100
				25 50 75 100
				25 50 75 100
				25 50 75 100
				25 50 75 100
				25 50 75 100
				25 50 75 100
				25 50 75 100
				25 50 75 100
				25 50 75 100
				25 50 75 100
				25 50 75 100

The 5-Minute Mindset

Step 4: Design a Plan
Brainstorm; Resources,
Principles, Rules and Guidelines

Goal / Due Date:

What resources of information are available to you? Do you know any experts? What are the hard and fast rules that will lead to success? What are the core principles? What guidelines are you going to set? How are you going to achieve your goal?

Priority	Entries

5 The -Minute Mindset

Step 4: Design a Plan
Step 5: Implement a Plan
Daily/Weekly Goal Tracker

Month_____

GOAL(S)

Daily/Weekly Tasks		Mon	Tue	Wed	Thur	Fri	Sat	Sun	Total	Achievement Bar
	Date									
	Goal									25 50 75 100
	Actual									
	Goal									25 50 75 100
	Actual									
	Goal									25 50 75 100
	Actual									
	Goal									25 50 75 100
	Actual									
	Goal									25 50 75 100
	Actual									
Daily/Weekly Tasks		Mon	Tue	Wed	Thur	Fri	Sat	Sun	Total	Achievement Bar
	Date									
	Goal									25 50 75 100
	Actual									
	Goal									25 50 75 100
	Actual									
	Goal									25 50 75 100
	Actual									
	Goal									25 50 75 100
	Actual									
	Goal									25 50 75 100
	Actual									
Daily/Weekly Tasks		Mon	Tue	Wed	Thur	Fri	Sat	Sun	Total	Achievement Bar
	Date									
	Goal									25 50 75 100
	Actual									
	Goal									25 50 75 100
	Actual									
	Goal									25 50 75 100
	Actual									
	Goal									25 50 75 100
	Actual									
	Goal									25 50 75 100
	Actual									

The 5-Minute Mindset

Step 4: Design a Plan
Step 5: Implement a Plan
Daily/Weekly Goal Tracker

Month_____

GOAL(S)

Daily/Weekly Tasks		Mon	Tue	Wed	Thur	Fri	Sat	Sun	Total	Achievement Bar
	Date									
	Goal									25 50 75 100
	Actual									
	Goal									25 50 75 100
	Actual									
	Goal									25 50 75 100
	Actual									
	Goal									25 50 75 100
	Actual									
	Goal									25 50 75 100
	Actual									

Daily/Weekly Tasks		Mon	Tue	Wed	Thur	Fri	Sat	Sun	Total	Achievement Bar
	Date									
	Goal									25 50 75 100
	Actual									
	Goal									25 50 75 100
	Actual									
	Goal									25 50 75 100
	Actual									
	Goal									25 50 75 100
	Actual									
	Goal									25 50 75 100
	Actual									

Daily/Weekly Tasks		Mon	Tue	Wed	Thur	Fri	Sat	Sun	Total	Achievement Bar
	Date									
	Goal									25 50 75 100
	Actual									
	Goal									25 50 75 100
	Actual									
	Goal									25 50 75 100
	Actual									
	Goal									25 50 75 100
	Actual									
	Goal									25 50 75 100
	Actual									

The 5-Minute Mindset

Step 4: Design a Plan
Step 5: Implement a Plan
Daily/Weekly Goal Tracker

Month_____

GOAL(S)

Daily/Weekly Tasks	Date	Mon	Tue	Wed	Thur	Fri	Sat	Sun	Total	Achievement Bar
	Goal									25 50 75 100
	Actual									
	Goal									25 50 75 100
	Actual									
	Goal									25 50 75 100
	Actual									
	Goal									25 50 75 100
	Actual									
	Goal									25 50 75 100
	Actual									

Daily/Weekly Tasks	Date	Mon	Tue	Wed	Thur	Fri	Sat	Sun	Total	Achievement Bar
	Goal									25 50 75 100
	Actual									
	Goal									25 50 75 100
	Actual									
	Goal									25 50 75 100
	Actual									
	Goal									25 50 75 100
	Actual									
	Goal									25 50 75 100
	Actual									

Daily/Weekly Tasks	Date	Mon	Tue	Wed	Thur	Fri	Sat	Sun	Total	Achievement Bar
	Goal									25 50 75 100
	Actual									
	Goal									25 50 75 100
	Actual									
	Goal									25 50 75 100
	Actual									
	Goal									25 50 75 100
	Actual									
	Goal									25 50 75 100
	Actual									

The 5-Minute Mindset

Step 4: Design a Plan
Step 5: Implement a Plan
Daily/Weekly Goal Tracker

Month_____

GOAL(S)

Daily/Weekly Tasks	Date	Mon	Tue	Wed	Thur	Fri	Sat	Sun	Total	Achievement Bar
	Goal									25 50 75 100
	Actual									
	Goal									25 50 75 100
	Actual									
	Goal									25 50 75 100
	Actual									
	Goal									25 50 75 100
	Actual									
	Goal									25 50 75 100
	Actual									

Daily/Weekly Tasks	Date	Mon	Tue	Wed	Thur	Fri	Sat	Sun	Total	Achievement Bar
	Goal									25 50 75 100
	Actual									
	Goal									25 50 75 100
	Actual									
	Goal									25 50 75 100
	Actual									
	Goal									25 50 75 100
	Actual									
	Goal									25 50 75 100
	Actual									

Daily/Weekly Tasks	Date	Mon	Tue	Wed	Thur	Fri	Sat	Sun	Total	Achievement Bar
	Goal									25 50 75 100
	Actual									
	Goal									25 50 75 100
	Actual									
	Goal									25 50 75 100
	Actual									
	Goal									25 50 75 100
	Actual									
	Goal									25 50 75 100
	Actual									

5-Minute Mindset

Step 4: Design a Plan
Step 5: Implement a Plan

Daily/Weekly Goal Tracker

Month_____

GOAL(S)

Daily/Weekly Tasks	Date	Mon	Tue	Wed	Thur	Fri	Sat	Sun	Total	Achievement Bar
	Goal									25 50 75 100
	Actual									
	Goal									25 50 75 100
	Actual									
	Goal									25 50 75 100
	Actual									
	Goal									25 50 75 100
	Actual									
	Goal									25 50 75 100
	Actual									

Daily/Weekly Tasks	Date	Mon	Tue	Wed	Thur	Fri	Sat	Sun	Total	Achievement Bar
	Goal									25 50 75 100
	Actual									
	Goal									25 50 75 100
	Actual									
	Goal									25 50 75 100
	Actual									
	Goal									25 50 75 100
	Actual									
	Goal									25 50 75 100
	Actual									

Daily/Weekly Tasks	Date	Mon	Tue	Wed	Thur	Fri	Sat	Sun	Total	Achievement Bar
	Goal									25 50 75 100
	Actual									
	Goal									25 50 75 100
	Actual									
	Goal									25 50 75 100
	Actual									
	Goal									25 50 75 100
	Actual									
	Goal									25 50 75 100
	Actual									

The 5-Minute Mindset

Step 4: Design a Plan
Step 5: Implement a Plan
Daily/Weekly Goal Tracker

Month_____

GOAL(S)

Daily/Weekly Tasks		Mon	Tue	Wed	Thur	Fri	Sat	Sun	Total	Achievement Bar
	Date									
	Goal									25 50 75 100
	Actual									
	Goal									25 50 75 100
	Actual									
	Goal									25 50 75 100
	Actual									
	Goal									25 50 75 100
	Actual									
	Goal									25 50 75 100
	Actual									
Daily/Weekly Tasks		Mon	Tue	Wed	Thur	Fri	Sat	Sun	Total	Achievement Bar
	Date									
	Goal									25 50 75 100
	Actual									
	Goal									25 50 75 100
	Actual									
	Goal									25 50 75 100
	Actual									
	Goal									25 50 75 100
	Actual									
	Goal									25 50 75 100
	Actual									
Daily/Weekly Tasks		Mon	Tue	Wed	Thur	Fri	Sat	Sun	Total	Achievement Bar
	Date									
	Goal									25 50 75 100
	Actual									
	Goal									25 50 75 100
	Actual									
	Goal									25 50 75 100
	Actual									
	Goal									25 50 75 100
	Actual									
	Goal									25 50 75 100
	Actual									

The 5-Minute Mindset

Step 4: Design a Plan
Step 5: Implement a Plan
Daily/Weekly Goal Tracker

Month_____

GOAL(S)

Daily/Weekly Tasks		Mon	Tue	Wed	Thur	Fri	Sat	Sun	Total	Achievement Bar
	Date									
	Goal									25 50 75 100
	Actual									
	Goal									25 50 75 100
	Actual									
	Goal									25 50 75 100
	Actual									
	Goal									25 50 75 100
	Actual									
	Goal									25 50 75 100
	Actual									

Daily/Weekly Tasks		Mon	Tue	Wed	Thur	Fri	Sat	Sun	Total	Achievement Bar
	Date									
	Goal									25 50 75 100
	Actual									
	Goal									25 50 75 100
	Actual									
	Goal									25 50 75 100
	Actual									
	Goal									25 50 75 100
	Actual									
	Goal									25 50 75 100
	Actual									

Daily/Weekly Tasks		Mon	Tue	Wed	Thur	Fri	Sat	Sun	Total	Achievement Bar
	Date									
	Goal									25 50 75 100
	Actual									
	Goal									25 50 75 100
	Actual									
	Goal									25 50 75 100
	Actual									
	Goal									25 50 75 100
	Actual									
	Goal									25 50 75 100
	Actual									

5-Minute Mindset

Step 4: Design a Plan
Step 5: Implement a Plan
Daily/Weekly Goal Tracker

Month_____

GOAL(S)

Daily/Weekly Tasks	Date	Mon	Tue	Wed	Thur	Fri	Sat	Sun	Total	Achievement Bar
	Goal									25 50 75 100
	Actual									
	Goal									25 50 75 100
	Actual									
	Goal									25 50 75 100
	Actual									
	Goal									25 50 75 100
	Actual									
	Goal									25 50 75 100
	Actual									

Daily/Weekly Tasks	Date	Mon	Tue	Wed	Thur	Fri	Sat	Sun	Total	Achievement Bar
	Goal									25 50 75 100
	Actual									
	Goal									25 50 75 100
	Actual									
	Goal									25 50 75 100
	Actual									
	Goal									25 50 75 100
	Actual									
	Goal									25 50 75 100
	Actual									

Daily/Weekly Tasks	Date	Mon	Tue	Wed	Thur	Fri	Sat	Sun	Total	Achievement Bar
	Goal									25 50 75 100
	Actual									
	Goal									25 50 75 100
	Actual									
	Goal									25 50 75 100
	Actual									
	Goal									25 50 75 100
	Actual									
	Goal									25 50 75 100
	Actual									

5-Minute Mindset The

Step 4: Design a Plan
Step 5: Implement a Plan
Daily/Weekly Goal Tracker

Month_____

GOAL(S)

Daily/Weekly Tasks	Date	Mon	Tue	Wed	Thur	Fri	Sat	Sun	Total	Achievement Bar
	Goal									25 50 75 100
	Actual									
	Goal									25 50 75 100
	Actual									
	Goal									25 50 75 100
	Actual									
	Goal									25 50 75 100
	Actual									
	Goal									25 50 75 100
	Actual									

Daily/Weekly Tasks	Date	Mon	Tue	Wed	Thur	Fri	Sat	Sun	Total	Achievement Bar
	Goal									25 50 75 100
	Actual									
	Goal									25 50 75 100
	Actual									
	Goal									25 50 75 100
	Actual									
	Goal									25 50 75 100
	Actual									
	Goal									25 50 75 100
	Actual									

Daily/Weekly Tasks	Date	Mon	Tue	Wed	Thur	Fri	Sat	Sun	Total	Achievement Bar
	Goal									25 50 75 100
	Actual									
	Goal									25 50 75 100
	Actual									
	Goal									25 50 75 100
	Actual									
	Goal									25 50 75 100
	Actual									
	Goal									25 50 75 100
	Actual									

5-Minute Mindset (The)

Step 4: Design a Plan
Step 5: Implement a Plan

Month_____

Daily/Weekly Goal Tracker

GOAL(S)

Daily/Weekly Tasks	Date	Mon	Tue	Wed	Thur	Fri	Sat	Sun	Total	Achievement Bar
	Goal									25 50 75 100
	Actual									
	Goal									25 50 75 100
	Actual									
	Goal									25 50 75 100
	Actual									
	Goal									25 50 75 100
	Actual									
	Goal									25 50 75 100
	Actual									

Daily/Weekly Tasks	Date	Mon	Tue	Wed	Thur	Fri	Sat	Sun	Total	Achievement Bar
	Goal									25 50 75 100
	Actual									
	Goal									25 50 75 100
	Actual									
	Goal									25 50 75 100
	Actual									
	Goal									25 50 75 100
	Actual									
	Goal									25 50 75 100
	Actual									

Daily/Weekly Tasks	Date	Mon	Tue	Wed	Thur	Fri	Sat	Sun	Total	Achievement Bar
	Goal									25 50 75 100
	Actual									
	Goal									25 50 75 100
	Actual									
	Goal									25 50 75 100
	Actual									
	Goal									25 50 75 100
	Actual									
	Goal									25 50 75 100
	Actual									

5-Minute Mindset

Step 4: Design a Plan
Step 5: Implement a Plan
Daily/Weekly Goal Tracker

Month_____

GOAL(S)

Daily/Weekly Tasks		Mon	Tue	Wed	Thur	Fri	Sat	Sun	Total	Achievement Bar
	Date									
	Goal									25 50 75 100
	Actual									
	Goal									25 50 75 100
	Actual									
	Goal									25 50 75 100
	Actual									
	Goal									25 50 75 100
	Actual									
	Goal									25 50 75 100
	Actual									

Daily/Weekly Tasks		Mon	Tue	Wed	Thur	Fri	Sat	Sun	Total	Achievement Bar
	Date									
	Goal									25 50 75 100
	Actual									
	Goal									25 50 75 100
	Actual									
	Goal									25 50 75 100
	Actual									
	Goal									25 50 75 100
	Actual									
	Goal									25 50 75 100
	Actual									

Daily/Weekly Tasks		Mon	Tue	Wed	Thur	Fri	Sat	Sun	Total	Achievement Bar
	Date									
	Goal									25 50 75 100
	Actual									
	Goal									25 50 75 100
	Actual									
	Goal									25 50 75 100
	Actual									
	Goal									25 50 75 100
	Actual									

The 5-Minute Mindset

Step 4: Design a Plan
Step 5: Implement a Plan
Daily/Weekly Goal Tracker

Month_____

GOAL(S)

Daily/Weekly Tasks		Mon	Tue	Wed	Thur	Fri	Sat	Sun	Total	Achievement Bar
	Date									
	Goal									25 50 75 100
	Actual									
	Goal									25 50 75 100
	Actual									
	Goal									25 50 75 100
	Actual									
	Goal									25 50 75 100
	Actual									
	Goal									25 50 75 100
	Actual									
Daily/Weekly Tasks		Mon	Tue	Wed	Thur	Fri	Sat	Sun	Total	Achievement Bar
	Date									
	Goal									25 50 75 100
	Actual									
	Goal									25 50 75 100
	Actual									
	Goal									25 50 75 100
	Actual									
	Goal									25 50 75 100
	Actual									
	Goal									25 50 75 100
	Actual									
Daily/Weekly Tasks		Mon	Tue	Wed	Thur	Fri	Sat	Sun	Total	Achievement Bar
	Date									
	Goal									25 50 75 100
	Actual									
	Goal									25 50 75 100
	Actual									
	Goal									25 50 75 100
	Actual									
	Goal									25 50 75 100
	Actual									
	Goal									25 50 75 100
	Actual									

The **5**-Minute Mindset	**Step 4: Design a Plan** **Step 5: Implement a Plan** Daily/Weekly Goal Tracker	**Month_____**

GOAL(S)

Daily/Weekly Tasks		Mon	Tue	Wed	Thur	Fri	Sat	Sun	Total	Achievement Bar
Daily/Weekly Tasks	**Date**									
	Goal									25 50 75 100
	Actual									
	Goal									25 50 75 100
	Actual									
	Goal									25 50 75 100
	Actual									
	Goal									25 50 75 100
	Actual									
	Goal									25 50 75 100
	Actual									

Daily/Weekly Tasks		Mon	Tue	Wed	Thur	Fri	Sat	Sun	Total	Achievement Bar
Daily/Weekly Tasks	**Date**									
	Goal									25 50 75 100
	Actual									
	Goal									25 50 75 100
	Actual									
	Goal									25 50 75 100
	Actual									
	Goal									25 50 75 100
	Actual									
	Goal									25 50 75 100
	Actual									

Daily/Weekly Tasks		Mon	Tue	Wed	Thur	Fri	Sat	Sun	Total	Achievement Bar
Daily/Weekly Tasks	**Date**									
	Goal									25 50 75 100
	Actual									
	Goal									25 50 75 100
	Actual									
	Goal									25 50 75 100
	Actual									
	Goal									25 50 75 100
	Actual									
	Goal									25 50 75 100
	Actual									

5-Minute Mindset

Step 4: Design a Plan
Step 5: Implement a Plan
Daily/Weekly Goal Tracker

Month_____

GOAL(S)

Daily/Weekly Tasks		Mon	Tue	Wed	Thur	Fri	Sat	Sun	Total	Achievement Bar
	Date									
	Goal									25 50 75 100
	Actual									
	Goal									25 50 75 100
	Actual									
	Goal									25 50 75 100
	Actual									
	Goal									25 50 75 100
	Actual									
	Goal									25 50 75 100
	Actual									

Daily/Weekly Tasks		Mon	Tue	Wed	Thur	Fri	Sat	Sun	Total	Achievement Bar
	Date									
	Goal									25 50 75 100
	Actual									
	Goal									25 50 75 100
	Actual									
	Goal									25 50 75 100
	Actual									
	Goal									25 50 75 100
	Actual									
	Goal									25 50 75 100
	Actual									

Daily/Weekly Tasks		Mon	Tue	Wed	Thur	Fri	Sat	Sun	Total	Achievement Bar
	Date									
	Goal									25 50 75 100
	Actual									
	Goal									25 50 75 100
	Actual									
	Goal									25 50 75 100
	Actual									
	Goal									25 50 75 100
	Actual									
	Goal									25 50 75 100
	Actual									

The 5-Minute Mindset

Step 4: Design a Plan
Step 5: Implement a Plan
Daily/Weekly Goal Tracker

Month_____

GOAL(S)

Daily/Weekly Tasks		Mon	Tue	Wed	Thur	Fri	Sat	Sun	Total	Achievement Bar
	Date									
	Goal									25 50 75 100
	Actual									
	Goal									25 50 75 100
	Actual									
	Goal									25 50 75 100
	Actual									
	Goal									25 50 75 100
	Actual									
	Goal									25 50 75 100
	Actual									

Daily/Weekly Tasks		Mon	Tue	Wed	Thur	Fri	Sat	Sun	Total	Achievement Bar
	Date									
	Goal									25 50 75 100
	Actual									
	Goal									25 50 75 100
	Actual									
	Goal									25 50 75 100
	Actual									
	Goal									25 50 75 100
	Actual									
	Goal									25 50 75 100
	Actual									

Daily/Weekly Tasks		Mon	Tue	Wed	Thur	Fri	Sat	Sun	Total	Achievement Bar
	Date									
	Goal									25 50 75 100
	Actual									
	Goal									25 50 75 100
	Actual									
	Goal									25 50 75 100
	Actual									
	Goal									25 50 75 100
	Actual									
	Goal									25 50 75 100
	Actual									

Step 4: Design a Plan
Step 5: Implement a Plan   Month_____

The 5-Minute Mindset

Daily/Weekly Goal Tracker

GOAL(S)

Daily/Weekly Tasks		Mon	Tue	Wed	Thur	Fri	Sat	Sun	Total	Achievement Bar
	Date									
	Goal									25 50 75 100
	Actual									
	Goal									25 50 75 100
	Actual									
	Goal									25 50 75 100
	Actual									
	Goal									25 50 75 100
	Actual									
	Goal									25 50 75 100
	Actual									

Daily/Weekly Tasks		Mon	Tue	Wed	Thur	Fri	Sat	Sun	Total	Achievement Bar
	Date									
	Goal									25 50 75 100
	Actual									
	Goal									25 50 75 100
	Actual									
	Goal									25 50 75 100
	Actual									
	Goal									25 50 75 100
	Actual									
	Goal									25 50 75 100
	Actual									

Daily/Weekly Tasks		Mon	Tue	Wed	Thur	Fri	Sat	Sun	Total	Achievement Bar
	Date									
	Goal									25 50 75 100
	Actual									
	Goal									25 50 75 100
	Actual									
	Goal									25 50 75 100
	Actual									
	Goal									25 50 75 100
	Actual									
	Goal									25 50 75 100
	Actual									

The 5-Minute Mindset

Step 4: Design a Plan
Step 5: Implement a Plan
Daily/Weekly Goal Tracker

Month_____

GOAL(S)

Daily/Weekly Tasks		Mon	Tue	Wed	Thur	Fri	Sat	Sun	Total	Achievement Bar
	Date									
	Goal									25 50 75 100
	Actual									
	Goal									25 50 75 100
	Actual									
	Goal									25 50 75 100
	Actual									
	Goal									25 50 75 100
	Actual									
	Goal									25 50 75 100
	Actual									

Daily/Weekly Tasks		Mon	Tue	Wed	Thur	Fri	Sat	Sun	Total	Achievement Bar
	Date									
	Goal									25 50 75 100
	Actual									
	Goal									25 50 75 100
	Actual									
	Goal									25 50 75 100
	Actual									
	Goal									25 50 75 100
	Actual									
	Goal									25 50 75 100
	Actual									

Daily/Weekly Tasks		Mon	Tue	Wed	Thur	Fri	Sat	Sun	Total	Achievement Bar
	Date									
	Goal									25 50 75 100
	Actual									
	Goal									25 50 75 100
	Actual									
	Goal									25 50 75 100
	Actual									
	Goal									25 50 75 100
	Actual									
	Goal									25 50 75 100
	Actual									

The 5-Minute Mindset

Step 4: Design a Plan
Step 5: Implement a Plan

Month_____

Daily/Weekly Goal Tracker

GOAL(S)

Daily/Weekly Tasks		Mon	Tue	Wed	Thur	Fri	Sat	Sun	Total	Achievement Bar
	Date									
	Goal									25 50 75 100
	Actual									
	Goal									25 50 75 100
	Actual									
	Goal									25 50 75 100
	Actual									
	Goal									25 50 75 100
	Actual									
	Goal									25 50 75 100
	Actual									

Daily/Weekly Tasks		Mon	Tue	Wed	Thur	Fri	Sat	Sun	Total	Achievement Bar
	Date									
	Goal									25 50 75 100
	Actual									
	Goal									25 50 75 100
	Actual									
	Goal									25 50 75 100
	Actual									
	Goal									25 50 75 100
	Actual									
	Goal									25 50 75 100
	Actual									

Daily/Weekly Tasks		Mon	Tue	Wed	Thur	Fri	Sat	Sun	Total	Achievement Bar
	Date									
	Goal									25 50 75 100
	Actual									
	Goal									25 50 75 100
	Actual									
	Goal									25 50 75 100
	Actual									
	Goal									25 50 75 100
	Actual									
	Goal									25 50 75 100
	Actual									

The 5-Minute Mindset

Step 6: Provide Ongoing Motivation
Step 7: Interpret Results and Adjust Accordingly
Step 8: Celebrate Your Success
Step 9: Arrive at Your Destination

Date	Entries

5The**-Minute Mindset**

Step 6: Provide Ongoing Motivation
Step 7: Interpret Results and Adjust Accordingly
Step 8: Celebrate Your Success
Step 9: Arrive at Your Destination

Date	Entries

The 5-Minute Mindset

Step 6: Provide Ongoing Motivation
Step 7: Interpret Results and Adjust Accordingly
Step 8: Celebrate Your Success
Step 9: Arrive at Your Destination

Date	Entries

The 5-Minute Mindset

Step 6: Provide Ongoing Motivation
Step 7: Interpret Results and Adjust Accordingly
Step 8: Celebrate Your Success
Step 9: Arrive at Your Destination

Date	Entries

The 5-Minute Mindset

Forms for # 2

**(After you decide what area you want to work
on, come back to this page and fill it in.)**

_____

_____

_____

The 5-Minute Mindset   **Step 1: Make A Decision**

What area do you want to work on?
(Example: Spiritual, Physical, Social, Emotional, Educational, Financial)

The 5-Minute Mindset

Step 2: Write Your Story and Find Your 'Whys'

What area in your life did you decide to work on?

**Make a list of your reasons for this decision or write stories
that illustrate why this decision is important to you.**

The 5-Minute Mindset

**Step 2: Write Your Story
and Find Your 'Whys'**

What area in your life did you decide to work on?

**Make a list of your reasons for this decision or write stories
that illustrate why this decision is important to you.**

The 5-Minute Mindset

Step 3: Set Goals
Long Term and Intermediate

Long Term Goal:	Deadline	Goal	Actual

Achievement Bar

| 25% | 50% | 75% | 100% |

Intermediate Goals or Tasks	Deadline	Goal	Actual	Achievement Bar
				25 50 75 100
				25 50 75 100
				25 50 75 100
				25 50 75 100
				25 50 75 100
				25 50 75 100
				25 50 75 100
				25 50 75 100
				25 50 75 100
				25 50 75 100
				25 50 75 100
				25 50 75 100
				25 50 75 100
				25 50 75 100
				25 50 75 100
				25 50 75 100
				25 50 75 100

5-Minute Mindset

Step 4: Design a Plan
Brainstorm; Resources,
Principles, Rules and Guidelines

Goal / Due Date:

What resources of information are available to you? Do you know any experts? What are the hard and fast rules that will lead to success? What are the core principles? What guidelines are you going to set? How are you going to achieve your goal?

Priority	Entries

5-Minute Mindset

Step 4: Design a Plan
Step 5: Implement a Plan
Daily/Weekly Goal Tracker

Month_____

GOAL(S)

Daily/Weekly Tasks		Mon	Tue	Wed	Thur	Fri	Sat	Sun	Total	Achievement Bar
	Date									
	Goal									25 50 75 100
	Actual									
	Goal									25 50 75 100
	Actual									
	Goal									25 50 75 100
	Actual									
	Goal									25 50 75 100
	Actual									
	Goal									25 50 75 100
	Actual									

Daily/Weekly Tasks		Mon	Tue	Wed	Thur	Fri	Sat	Sun	Total	Achievement Bar
	Date									
	Goal									25 50 75 100
	Actual									
	Goal									25 50 75 100
	Actual									
	Goal									25 50 75 100
	Actual									
	Goal									25 50 75 100
	Actual									
	Goal									25 50 75 100
	Actual									

Daily/Weekly Tasks		Mon	Tue	Wed	Thur	Fri	Sat	Sun	Total	Achievement Bar
	Date									
	Goal									25 50 75 100
	Actual									
	Goal									25 50 75 100
	Actual									
	Goal									25 50 75 100
	Actual									
	Goal									25 50 75 100
	Actual									
	Goal									25 50 75 100
	Actual									

5-Minute Mindset

Step 4: Design a Plan
Step 5: Implement a Plan
Daily/Weekly Goal Tracker

Month_____

GOAL(S)

Daily/Weekly Tasks		Mon	Tue	Wed	Thur	Fri	Sat	Sun	Total	Achievement Bar
	Date									
	Goal									25 50 75 100
	Actual									
	Goal									25 50 75 100
	Actual									
	Goal									25 50 75 100
	Actual									
	Goal									25 50 75 100
	Actual									
	Goal									25 50 75 100
	Actual									

Daily/Weekly Tasks		Mon	Tue	Wed	Thur	Fri	Sat	Sun	Total	Achievement Bar
	Date									
	Goal									25 50 75 100
	Actual									
	Goal									25 50 75 100
	Actual									
	Goal									25 50 75 100
	Actual									
	Goal									25 50 75 100
	Actual									
	Goal									25 50 75 100
	Actual									

Daily/Weekly Tasks		Mon	Tue	Wed	Thur	Fri	Sat	Sun	Total	Achievement Bar
	Date									
	Goal									25 50 75 100
	Actual									
	Goal									25 50 75 100
	Actual									
	Goal									25 50 75 100
	Actual									
	Goal									25 50 75 100
	Actual									
	Goal									25 50 75 100
	Actual									

The 5-Minute Mindset

Step 4: Design a Plan
Step 5: Implement a Plan
Daily/Weekly Goal Tracker

Month_____

GOAL(S)

Daily/Weekly Tasks	Date	Mon	Tue	Wed	Thur	Fri	Sat	Sun	Total	Achievement Bar
	Goal									25 50 75 100
	Actual									
	Goal									25 50 75 100
	Actual									
	Goal									25 50 75 100
	Actual									
	Goal									25 50 75 100
	Actual									
	Goal									25 50 75 100
	Actual									

Daily/Weekly Tasks	Date	Mon	Tue	Wed	Thur	Fri	Sat	Sun	Total	Achievement Bar
	Goal									25 50 75 100
	Actual									
	Goal									25 50 75 100
	Actual									
	Goal									25 50 75 100
	Actual									
	Goal									25 50 75 100
	Actual									
	Goal									25 50 75 100
	Actual									

Daily/Weekly Tasks	Date	Mon	Tue	Wed	Thur	Fri	Sat	Sun	Total	Achievement Bar
	Goal									25 50 75 100
	Actual									
	Goal									25 50 75 100
	Actual									
	Goal									25 50 75 100
	Actual									
	Goal									25 50 75 100
	Actual									
	Goal									25 50 75 100
	Actual									

5 The -Minute Mindset

Step 4: Design a Plan
Step 5: Implement a Plan
Daily/Weekly Goal Tracker

Month_____

GOAL(S)

Daily/Weekly Tasks		Mon	Tue	Wed	Thur	Fri	Sat	Sun	Total	Achievement Bar
	Date									
	Goal									25 50 75 100
	Actual									
	Goal									25 50 75 100
	Actual									
	Goal									25 50 75 100
	Actual									
	Goal									25 50 75 100
	Actual									
	Goal									25 50 75 100
	Actual									

Daily/Weekly Tasks		Mon	Tue	Wed	Thur	Fri	Sat	Sun	Total	Achievement Bar
	Date									
	Goal									25 50 75 100
	Actual									
	Goal									25 50 75 100
	Actual									
	Goal									25 50 75 100
	Actual									
	Goal									25 50 75 100
	Actual									
	Goal									25 50 75 100
	Actual									

Daily/Weekly Tasks		Mon	Tue	Wed	Thur	Fri	Sat	Sun	Total	Achievement Bar
	Date									
	Goal									25 50 75 100
	Actual									
	Goal									25 50 75 100
	Actual									
	Goal									25 50 75 100
	Actual									
	Goal									25 50 75 100
	Actual									
	Goal									25 50 75 100
	Actual									

5-The Minute Mindset

Step 4: Design a Plan
Step 5: Implement a Plan

Month_____

Daily/Weekly Goal Tracker

GOAL(S)

Daily/Weekly Tasks		Mon	Tue	Wed	Thur	Fri	Sat	Sun	Total	Achievement Bar
	Date									
	Goal									25 50 75 100
	Actual									
	Goal									25 50 75 100
	Actual									
	Goal									25 50 75 100
	Actual									
	Goal									25 50 75 100
	Actual									
	Goal									25 50 75 100
	Actual									

Daily/Weekly Tasks		Mon	Tue	Wed	Thur	Fri	Sat	Sun	Total	Achievement Bar
	Date									
	Goal									25 50 75 100
	Actual									
	Goal									25 50 75 100
	Actual									
	Goal									25 50 75 100
	Actual									
	Goal									25 50 75 100
	Actual									
	Goal									25 50 75 100
	Actual									

Daily/Weekly Tasks		Mon	Tue	Wed	Thur	Fri	Sat	Sun	Total	Achievement Bar
	Date									
	Goal									25 50 75 100
	Actual									
	Goal									25 50 75 100
	Actual									
	Goal									25 50 75 100
	Actual									
	Goal									25 50 75 100
	Actual									
	Goal									25 50 75 100
	Actual									

Step 4: Design a Plan
Step 5: Implement a Plan

Month_____

The 5-Minute Mindset

Daily/Weekly Goal Tracker

GOAL(S)

Daily/Weekly Tasks		Mon	Tue	Wed	Thur	Fri	Sat	Sun	Total	Achievement Bar
	Date									
	Goal									25 50 75 100
	Actual									
	Goal									25 50 75 100
	Actual									
	Goal									25 50 75 100
	Actual									
	Goal									25 50 75 100
	Actual									
	Goal									25 50 75 100
	Actual									

Daily/Weekly Tasks		Mon	Tue	Wed	Thur	Fri	Sat	Sun	Total	Achievement Bar
	Date									
	Goal									25 50 75 100
	Actual									
	Goal									25 50 75 100
	Actual									
	Goal									25 50 75 100
	Actual									
	Goal									25 50 75 100
	Actual									
	Goal									25 50 75 100
	Actual									

Daily/Weekly Tasks		Mon	Tue	Wed	Thur	Fri	Sat	Sun	Total	Achievement Bar
	Date									
	Goal									25 50 75 100
	Actual									
	Goal									25 50 75 100
	Actual									
	Goal									25 50 75 100
	Actual									
	Goal									25 50 75 100
	Actual									
	Goal									25 50 75 100
	Actual									

The 5-Minute Mindset

Step 4: Design a Plan
Step 5: Implement a Plan
Daily/Weekly Goal Tracker

Month_____

GOAL(S)

Daily/Weekly Tasks		Mon	Tue	Wed	Thur	Fri	Sat	Sun	Total	Achievement Bar
	Date									
	Goal									25 50 75 100
	Actual									
	Goal									25 50 75 100
	Actual									
	Goal									25 50 75 100
	Actual									
	Goal									25 50 75 100
	Actual									
	Goal									25 50 75 100
	Actual									

Daily/Weekly Tasks		Mon	Tue	Wed	Thur	Fri	Sat	Sun	Total	Achievement Bar
	Date									
	Goal									25 50 75 100
	Actual									
	Goal									25 50 75 100
	Actual									
	Goal									25 50 75 100
	Actual									
	Goal									25 50 75 100
	Actual									
	Goal									25 50 75 100
	Actual									

Daily/Weekly Tasks		Mon	Tue	Wed	Thur	Fri	Sat	Sun	Total	Achievement Bar
	Date									
	Goal									25 50 75 100
	Actual									
	Goal									25 50 75 100
	Actual									
	Goal									25 50 75 100
	Actual									
	Goal									25 50 75 100
	Actual									
	Goal									25 50 75 100
	Actual									

					Step 4: Design a Plan					

5 The Minute Mindset

Step 4: Design a Plan
Step 5: Implement a Plan
Daily/Weekly Goal Tracker

Month_____

GOAL(S)

Daily/Weekly Tasks		Mon	Tue	Wed	Thur	Fri	Sat	Sun	Total	Achievement Bar
	Date									
	Goal									25 50 75 100
	Actual									
	Goal									25 50 75 100
	Actual									
	Goal									25 50 75 100
	Actual									
	Goal									25 50 75 100
	Actual									
	Goal									25 50 75 100
	Actual									
Daily/Weekly Tasks		Mon	Tue	Wed	Thur	Fri	Sat	Sun	Total	Achievement Bar
	Date									
	Goal									25 50 75 100
	Actual									
	Goal									25 50 75 100
	Actual									
	Goal									25 50 75 100
	Actual									
	Goal									25 50 75 100
	Actual									
	Goal									25 50 75 100
	Actual									
Daily/Weekly Tasks		Mon	Tue	Wed	Thur	Fri	Sat	Sun	Total	Achievement Bar
	Date									
	Goal									25 50 75 100
	Actual									
	Goal									25 50 75 100
	Actual									
	Goal									25 50 75 100
	Actual									
	Goal									25 50 75 100
	Actual									
	Goal									25 50 75 100
	Actual									

5 The -Minute Mindset

Step 4: Design a Plan
Step 5: Implement a Plan
Daily/Weekly Goal Tracker

Month_____

GOAL(S)

Daily/Weekly Tasks	Date	Mon	Tue	Wed	Thur	Fri	Sat	Sun	Total	Achievement Bar
	Goal									25 50 75 100
	Actual									
	Goal									25 50 75 100
	Actual									
	Goal									25 50 75 100
	Actual									
	Goal									25 50 75 100
	Actual									
	Goal									25 50 75 100
	Actual									

Daily/Weekly Tasks	Date	Mon	Tue	Wed	Thur	Fri	Sat	Sun	Total	Achievement Bar
	Goal									25 50 75 100
	Actual									
	Goal									25 50 75 100
	Actual									
	Goal									25 50 75 100
	Actual									
	Goal									25 50 75 100
	Actual									
	Goal									25 50 75 100
	Actual									

Daily/Weekly Tasks	Date	Mon	Tue	Wed	Thur	Fri	Sat	Sun	Total	Achievement Bar
	Goal									25 50 75 100
	Actual									
	Goal									25 50 75 100
	Actual									
	Goal									25 50 75 100
	Actual									
	Goal									25 50 75 100
	Actual									

5-Minute Mindset

Step 4: Design a Plan
Step 5: Implement a Plan

Daily/Weekly Goal Tracker

Month_____

GOAL(S)

Daily/Weekly Tasks		Mon	Tue	Wed	Thur	Fri	Sat	Sun	Total	Achievement Bar
	Date									
	Goal									25 50 75 100
	Actual									
	Goal									25 50 75 100
	Actual									
	Goal									25 50 75 100
	Actual									
	Goal									25 50 75 100
	Actual									
	Goal									25 50 75 100
	Actual									

Daily/Weekly Tasks		Mon	Tue	Wed	Thur	Fri	Sat	Sun	Total	Achievement Bar
	Date									
	Goal									25 50 75 100
	Actual									
	Goal									25 50 75 100
	Actual									
	Goal									25 50 75 100
	Actual									
	Goal									25 50 75 100
	Actual									
	Goal									25 50 75 100
	Actual									

Daily/Weekly Tasks		Mon	Tue	Wed	Thur	Fri	Sat	Sun	Total	Achievement Bar
	Date									
	Goal									25 50 75 100
	Actual									
	Goal									25 50 75 100
	Actual									
	Goal									25 50 75 100
	Actual									
	Goal									25 50 75 100
	Actual									
	Goal									25 50 75 100
	Actual									

The 5-Minute Mindset

Step 4: Design a Plan
Step 5: Implement a Plan
Daily/Weekly Goal Tracker

Month_____

GOAL(S)

Daily/Weekly Tasks	Date	Mon	Tue	Wed	Thur	Fri	Sat	Sun	Total	Achievement Bar
	Goal									25 50 75 100
	Actual									
	Goal									25 50 75 100
	Actual									
	Goal									25 50 75 100
	Actual									
	Goal									25 50 75 100
	Actual									
	Goal									25 50 75 100
	Actual									

Daily/Weekly Tasks	Date	Mon	Tue	Wed	Thur	Fri	Sat	Sun	Total	Achievement Bar
	Goal									25 50 75 100
	Actual									
	Goal									25 50 75 100
	Actual									
	Goal									25 50 75 100
	Actual									
	Goal									25 50 75 100
	Actual									
	Goal									25 50 75 100
	Actual									

Daily/Weekly Tasks	Date	Mon	Tue	Wed	Thur	Fri	Sat	Sun	Total	Achievement Bar
	Goal									25 50 75 100
	Actual									
	Goal									25 50 75 100
	Actual									
	Goal									25 50 75 100
	Actual									
	Goal									25 50 75 100
	Actual									
	Goal									25 50 75 100
	Actual									

5 The -Minute Mindset

Step 4: Design a Plan
Step 5: Implement a Plan
Daily/Weekly Goal Tracker

Month_____

GOAL(S)

Daily/Weekly Tasks	Date	Mon	Tue	Wed	Thur	Fri	Sat	Sun	Total	Achievement Bar
	Goal									25 50 75 100
	Actual									
	Goal									25 50 75 100
	Actual									
	Goal									25 50 75 100
	Actual									
	Goal									25 50 75 100
	Actual									
	Goal									25 50 75 100
	Actual									

Daily/Weekly Tasks	Date	Mon	Tue	Wed	Thur	Fri	Sat	Sun	Total	Achievement Bar
	Goal									25 50 75 100
	Actual									
	Goal									25 50 75 100
	Actual									
	Goal									25 50 75 100
	Actual									
	Goal									25 50 75 100
	Actual									
	Goal									25 50 75 100
	Actual									

Daily/Weekly Tasks	Date	Mon	Tue	Wed	Thur	Fri	Sat	Sun	Total	Achievement Bar
	Goal									25 50 75 100
	Actual									
	Goal									25 50 75 100
	Actual									
	Goal									25 50 75 100
	Actual									
	Goal									25 50 75 100
	Actual									
	Goal									25 50 75 100
	Actual									

5-Minute Mindset (The)

Step 4: Design a Plan
Step 5: Implement a Plan
Daily/Weekly Goal Tracker

Month_____

GOAL(S)

Daily/Weekly Tasks		Mon	Tue	Wed	Thur	Fri	Sat	Sun	Total	Achievement Bar
	Date									
	Goal									25 50 75 100
	Actual									
	Goal									25 50 75 100
	Actual									
	Goal									25 50 75 100
	Actual									
	Goal									25 50 75 100
	Actual									
	Goal									25 50 75 100
	Actual									

Daily/Weekly Tasks		Mon	Tue	Wed	Thur	Fri	Sat	Sun	Total	Achievement Bar
	Date									
	Goal									25 50 75 100
	Actual									
	Goal									25 50 75 100
	Actual									
	Goal									25 50 75 100
	Actual									
	Goal									25 50 75 100
	Actual									
	Goal									25 50 75 100
	Actual									

Daily/Weekly Tasks		Mon	Tue	Wed	Thur	Fri	Sat	Sun	Total	Achievement Bar
	Date									
	Goal									25 50 75 100
	Actual									
	Goal									25 50 75 100
	Actual									
	Goal									25 50 75 100
	Actual									
	Goal									25 50 75 100
	Actual									
	Goal									25 50 75 100
	Actual									

5-Minute Mindset

Step 4: Design a Plan
Step 5: Implement a Plan
Daily/Weekly Goal Tracker

Month_____

GOAL(S)

Daily/Weekly Tasks	Date	Mon	Tue	Wed	Thur	Fri	Sat	Sun	Total	Achievement Bar
	Goal									25 50 75 100
	Actual									
	Goal									25 50 75 100
	Actual									
	Goal									25 50 75 100
	Actual									
	Goal									25 50 75 100
	Actual									
	Goal									25 50 75 100
	Actual									

Daily/Weekly Tasks	Date	Mon	Tue	Wed	Thur	Fri	Sat	Sun	Total	Achievement Bar
	Goal									25 50 75 100
	Actual									
	Goal									25 50 75 100
	Actual									
	Goal									25 50 75 100
	Actual									
	Goal									25 50 75 100
	Actual									
	Goal									25 50 75 100
	Actual									

Daily/Weekly Tasks	Date	Mon	Tue	Wed	Thur	Fri	Sat	Sun	Total	Achievement Bar
	Goal									25 50 75 100
	Actual									
	Goal									25 50 75 100
	Actual									
	Goal									25 50 75 100
	Actual									
	Goal									25 50 75 100
	Actual									
	Goal									25 50 75 100
	Actual									

The 5-Minute Mindset

Step 4: Design a Plan
Step 5: Implement a Plan
Daily/Weekly Goal Tracker

Month_____

GOAL(S)

Daily/Weekly Tasks		Mon	Tue	Wed	Thur	Fri	Sat	Sun	Total	Achievement Bar
	Date									
	Goal									25 50 75 100
	Actual									
	Goal									25 50 75 100
	Actual									
	Goal									25 50 75 100
	Actual									
	Goal									25 50 75 100
	Actual									
	Goal									25 50 75 100
	Actual									
Daily/Weekly Tasks		Mon	Tue	Wed	Thur	Fri	Sat	Sun	Total	Achievement Bar
	Date									
	Goal									25 50 75 100
	Actual									
	Goal									25 50 75 100
	Actual									
	Goal									25 50 75 100
	Actual									
	Goal									25 50 75 100
	Actual									
	Goal									25 50 75 100
	Actual									
Daily/Weekly Tasks		Mon	Tue	Wed	Thur	Fri	Sat	Sun	Total	Achievement Bar
	Date									
	Goal									25 50 75 100
	Actual									
	Goal									25 50 75 100
	Actual									
	Goal									25 50 75 100
	Actual									
	Goal									25 50 75 100
	Actual									
	Goal									25 50 75 100
	Actual									

5-Minute Mindset

Step 4: Design a Plan
Step 5: Implement a Plan

Daily/Weekly Goal Tracker

Month_____

GOAL(S)

Daily/Weekly Tasks		Mon	Tue	Wed	Thur	Fri	Sat	Sun	Total	Achievement Bar
	Date									
	Goal									25 50 75 100
	Actual									
	Goal									25 50 75 100
	Actual									
	Goal									25 50 75 100
	Actual									
	Goal									25 50 75 100
	Actual									
	Goal									25 50 75 100
	Actual									

Daily/Weekly Tasks		Mon	Tue	Wed	Thur	Fri	Sat	Sun	Total	Achievement Bar
	Date									
	Goal									25 50 75 100
	Actual									
	Goal									25 50 75 100
	Actual									
	Goal									25 50 75 100
	Actual									
	Goal									25 50 75 100
	Actual									
	Goal									25 50 75 100
	Actual									

Daily/Weekly Tasks		Mon	Tue	Wed	Thur	Fri	Sat	Sun	Total	Achievement Bar
	Date									
	Goal									25 50 75 100
	Actual									
	Goal									25 50 75 100
	Actual									
	Goal									25 50 75 100
	Actual									
	Goal									25 50 75 100
	Actual									
	Goal									25 50 75 100
	Actual									

5-Minute Mindset

Step 4: Design a Plan
Step 5: Implement a Plan

Month_____

Daily/Weekly Goal Tracker

GOAL(S)

Daily/Weekly Tasks		Mon	Tue	Wed	Thur	Fri	Sat	Sun	Total	Achievement Bar
	Date									
	Goal									25 50 75 100
	Actual									
	Goal									25 50 75 100
	Actual									
	Goal									25 50 75 100
	Actual									
	Goal									25 50 75 100
	Actual									
	Goal									25 50 75 100
	Actual									
Daily/Weekly Tasks		Mon	Tue	Wed	Thur	Fri	Sat	Sun	Total	Achievement Bar
	Date									
	Goal									25 50 75 100
	Actual									
	Goal									25 50 75 100
	Actual									
	Goal									25 50 75 100
	Actual									
	Goal									25 50 75 100
	Actual									
	Goal									25 50 75 100
	Actual									
Daily/Weekly Tasks		Mon	Tue	Wed	Thur	Fri	Sat	Sun	Total	Achievement Bar
	Date									
	Goal									25 50 75 100
	Actual									
	Goal									25 50 75 100
	Actual									
	Goal									25 50 75 100
	Actual									
	Goal									25 50 75 100
	Actual									
	Goal									25 50 75 100
	Actual									

5-Minute Mindset

Step 4: Design a Plan
Step 5: Implement a Plan
Daily/Weekly Goal Tracker

Month_____

GOAL(S)

Daily/Weekly Tasks		Mon	Tue	Wed	Thur	Fri	Sat	Sun	Total	Achievement Bar
	Date									
	Goal									25 50 75 100
	Actual									
	Goal									25 50 75 100
	Actual									
	Goal									25 50 75 100
	Actual									
	Goal									25 50 75 100
	Actual									
	Goal									25 50 75 100
	Actual									

Daily/Weekly Tasks		Mon	Tue	Wed	Thur	Fri	Sat	Sun	Total	Achievement Bar
	Date									
	Goal									25 50 75 100
	Actual									
	Goal									25 50 75 100
	Actual									
	Goal									25 50 75 100
	Actual									
	Goal									25 50 75 100
	Actual									
	Goal									25 50 75 100
	Actual									

Daily/Weekly Tasks		Mon	Tue	Wed	Thur	Fri	Sat	Sun	Total	Achievement Bar
	Date									
	Goal									25 50 75 100
	Actual									
	Goal									25 50 75 100
	Actual									
	Goal									25 50 75 100
	Actual									
	Goal									25 50 75 100
	Actual									
	Goal									25 50 75 100
	Actual									

The 5-Minute Mindset

Step 6: Provide Ongoing Motivation
Step 7: Interpret Results and Adjust Accordingly
Step 8: Celebrate Your Success
Step 9: Arrive at Your Destination

Date	Entries

The 5-Minute Mindset

Step 6: Provide Ongoing Motivation
Step 7: Interpret Results and Adjust Accordingly
Step 8: Celebrate Your Success
Step 9: Arrive at Your Destination

Date	Entries

The 5-Minute Mindset

Step 6: Provide Ongoing Motivation
Step 7: Interpret Results and Adjust Accordingly
Step 8: Celebrate Your Success
Step 9: Arrive at Your Destination

Date	Entries

The
5-Minute
Mindset

Step 6: Provide Ongoing Motivation
Step 7: Interpret Results and Adjust Accordingly
Step 8: Celebrate Your Success
Step 9: Arrive at Your Destination

Date	Entries

The 5-Minute Mindset

Forms for # 3

(After you decide what area you want to work on, come back to this page and fill it in.)

_____

_____

_____

The 5-Minute Mindset

Step 1: Make A Decision

What area do you want to work on?
(Example: Spiritual, Physical, Social, Emotional, Educational, Financial)

The 5-Minute Mindset   **Step 2: Write Your Story**
and Find Your 'Whys'

What area in your life did you decide to work on?

Make a list of your reasons for this decision or write stories
that illustrate why this decision is important to you.

The 5-Minute Mindset

Step 2: Write Your Story
and Find Your 'Whys'

What area in your life did you decide to work on?

**Make a list of your reasons for this decision or write stories
that illustrate why this decision is important to you.**

5 The Minute Mindset

Step 3: Set Goals
Long Term and Intermediate

Long Term Goal:	Deadline	Goal	Actual

Achievement Bar

25%   50%   75%   100%

Intermediate Goals or Tasks	Deadline	Goal	Actual	Achievement Bar
				25 50 75 100
				25 50 75 100
				25 50 75 100
				25 50 75 100
				25 50 75 100
				25 50 75 100
				25 50 75 100
				25 50 75 100
				25 50 75 100
				25 50 75 100
				25 50 75 100
				25 50 75 100
				25 50 75 100
				25 50 75 100
				25 50 75 100
				25 50 75 100
				25 50 75 100
				25 50 75 100

The 5-Minute Mindset

Step 4: Design a Plan
Brainstorm; Resources,
Principles, Rules and Guidelines

Goal / Due Date:

What resources of information are available to you? Do you know any experts? What are
the hard and fast rules that will lead to success? What are the core principles? What
guidelines are you going to set? How are you going to achieve your goal?

Priority	Entries

<table>
<tr><td rowspan="2">**5-Minute Mindset** ^{The}</td><td colspan="2">**Step 4: Design a Plan**
Step 5: Implement a Plan
Daily/Weekly Goal Tracker</td><td>**Month**_____</td></tr>
</table>

GOAL(S)

Daily/Weekly Tasks	Date	Mon	Tue	Wed	Thur	Fri	Sat	Sun	Total	Achievement Bar
	Goal									25 50 75 100
	Actual									
	Goal									25 50 75 100
	Actual									
	Goal									25 50 75 100
	Actual									
	Goal									25 50 75 100
	Actual									
	Goal									25 50 75 100
	Actual									

Daily/Weekly Tasks	Date	Mon	Tue	Wed	Thur	Fri	Sat	Sun	Total	Achievement Bar
	Goal									25 50 75 100
	Actual									
	Goal									25 50 75 100
	Actual									
	Goal									25 50 75 100
	Actual									
	Goal									25 50 75 100
	Actual									
	Goal									25 50 75 100
	Actual									

Daily/Weekly Tasks	Date	Mon	Tue	Wed	Thur	Fri	Sat	Sun	Total	Achievement Bar
	Goal									25 50 75 100
	Actual									
	Goal									25 50 75 100
	Actual									
	Goal									25 50 75 100
	Actual									
	Goal									25 50 75 100
	Actual									
	Goal									25 50 75 100
	Actual									

The 5-Minute Mindset

Step 4: Design a Plan
Step 5: Implement a Plan

Daily/Weekly Goal Tracker

Month_____

GOAL(S)

Daily/Weekly Tasks		Mon	Tue	Wed	Thur	Fri	Sat	Sun	Total	Achievement Bar
	Date									
	Goal									25 50 75 100
	Actual									
	Goal									25 50 75 100
	Actual									
	Goal									25 50 75 100
	Actual									
	Goal									25 50 75 100
	Actual									
	Goal									25 50 75 100
	Actual									

Daily/Weekly Tasks		Mon	Tue	Wed	Thur	Fri	Sat	Sun	Total	Achievement Bar
	Date									
	Goal									25 50 75 100
	Actual									
	Goal									25 50 75 100
	Actual									
	Goal									25 50 75 100
	Actual									
	Goal									25 50 75 100
	Actual									
	Goal									25 50 75 100
	Actual									

Daily/Weekly Tasks		Mon	Tue	Wed	Thur	Fri	Sat	Sun	Total	Achievement Bar
	Date									
	Goal									25 50 75 100
	Actual									
	Goal									25 50 75 100
	Actual									
	Goal									25 50 75 100
	Actual									
	Goal									25 50 75 100
	Actual									
	Goal									25 50 75 100
	Actual									

The 5-Minute Mindset

Step 4: Design a Plan
Step 5: Implement a Plan
Daily/Weekly Goal Tracker

Month_____

GOAL(S)

Daily/Weekly Tasks		Mon	Tue	Wed	Thur	Fri	Sat	Sun	Total	Achievement Bar
	Date									
	Goal									25 50 75 100
	Actual									
	Goal									25 50 75 100
	Actual									
	Goal									25 50 75 100
	Actual									
	Goal									25 50 75 100
	Actual									
	Goal									25 50 75 100
	Actual									

Daily/Weekly Tasks		Mon	Tue	Wed	Thur	Fri	Sat	Sun	Total	Achievement Bar
	Date									
	Goal									25 50 75 100
	Actual									
	Goal									25 50 75 100
	Actual									
	Goal									25 50 75 100
	Actual									
	Goal									25 50 75 100
	Actual									
	Goal									25 50 75 100
	Actual									

Daily/Weekly Tasks		Mon	Tue	Wed	Thur	Fri	Sat	Sun	Total	Achievement Bar
	Date									
	Goal									25 50 75 100
	Actual									
	Goal									25 50 75 100
	Actual									
	Goal									25 50 75 100
	Actual									
	Goal									25 50 75 100
	Actual									
	Goal									25 50 75 100
	Actual									

The 5-Minute Mindset

Step 4: Design a Plan
Step 5: Implement a Plan
Daily/Weekly Goal Tracker

Month_____

GOAL(S)

Daily/Weekly Tasks	Date	Mon	Tue	Wed	Thur	Fri	Sat	Sun	Total	Achievement Bar
	Goal									25 50 75 100
	Actual									
	Goal									25 50 75 100
	Actual									
	Goal									25 50 75 100
	Actual									
	Goal									25 50 75 100
	Actual									
	Goal									25 50 75 100
	Actual									

Daily/Weekly Tasks	Date	Mon	Tue	Wed	Thur	Fri	Sat	Sun	Total	Achievement Bar
	Goal									25 50 75 100
	Actual									
	Goal									25 50 75 100
	Actual									
	Goal									25 50 75 100
	Actual									
	Goal									25 50 75 100
	Actual									
	Goal									25 50 75 100
	Actual									

Daily/Weekly Tasks	Date	Mon	Tue	Wed	Thur	Fri	Sat	Sun	Total	Achievement Bar
	Goal									25 50 75 100
	Actual									
	Goal									25 50 75 100
	Actual									
	Goal									25 50 75 100
	Actual									
	Goal									25 50 75 100
	Actual									
	Goal									25 50 75 100
	Actual									

5-Minute Mindset

Step 4: Design a Plan
Step 5: Implement a Plan
Daily/Weekly Goal Tracker

Month_____

GOAL(S)

Daily/Weekly Tasks		Mon	Tue	Wed	Thur	Fri	Sat	Sun	Total	Achievement Bar
	Date									
	Goal									25 50 75 100
	Actual									
	Goal									25 50 75 100
	Actual									
	Goal									25 50 75 100
	Actual									
	Goal									25 50 75 100
	Actual									
	Goal									25 50 75 100
	Actual									
Daily/Weekly Tasks		Mon	Tue	Wed	Thur	Fri	Sat	Sun	Total	Achievement Bar
	Date									
	Goal									25 50 75 100
	Actual									
	Goal									25 50 75 100
	Actual									
	Goal									25 50 75 100
	Actual									
	Goal									25 50 75 100
	Actual									
	Goal									25 50 75 100
	Actual									
Daily/Weekly Tasks		Mon	Tue	Wed	Thur	Fri	Sat	Sun	Total	Achievement Bar
	Date									
	Goal									25 50 75 100
	Actual									
	Goal									25 50 75 100
	Actual									
	Goal									25 50 75 100
	Actual									
	Goal									25 50 75 100
	Actual									
	Goal									25 50 75 100
	Actual									

The 5-Minute Mindset

Step 4: Design a Plan
Step 5: Implement a Plan
Daily/Weekly Goal Tracker

Month_____

GOAL(S)

Daily/Weekly Tasks		Mon	Tue	Wed	Thur	Fri	Sat	Sun	Total	Achievement Bar
	Date									
	Goal									25 50 75 100
	Actual									
	Goal									25 50 75 100
	Actual									
	Goal									25 50 75 100
	Actual									
	Goal									25 50 75 100
	Actual									
	Goal									25 50 75 100
	Actual									

Daily/Weekly Tasks		Mon	Tue	Wed	Thur	Fri	Sat	Sun	Total	Achievement Bar
	Date									
	Goal									25 50 75 100
	Actual									
	Goal									25 50 75 100
	Actual									
	Goal									25 50 75 100
	Actual									
	Goal									25 50 75 100
	Actual									
	Goal									25 50 75 100
	Actual									

Daily/Weekly Tasks		Mon	Tue	Wed	Thur	Fri	Sat	Sun	Total	Achievement Bar
	Date									
	Goal									25 50 75 100
	Actual									
	Goal									25 50 75 100
	Actual									
	Goal									25 50 75 100
	Actual									
	Goal									25 50 75 100
	Actual									
	Goal									25 50 75 100
	Actual									

5-Minute Mindset (The)

Step 4: Design a Plan
Step 5: Implement a Plan   Month_____
Daily/Weekly Goal Tracker

GOAL(S)

Daily/Weekly Tasks	Date	Mon	Tue	Wed	Thur	Fri	Sat	Sun	Total	Achievement Bar
	Goal									25 50 75 100
	Actual									
	Goal									25 50 75 100
	Actual									
	Goal									25 50 75 100
	Actual									
	Goal									25 50 75 100
	Actual									
	Goal									25 50 75 100
	Actual									

Daily/Weekly Tasks	Date	Mon	Tue	Wed	Thur	Fri	Sat	Sun	Total	Achievement Bar
	Goal									25 50 75 100
	Actual									
	Goal									25 50 75 100
	Actual									
	Goal									25 50 75 100
	Actual									
	Goal									25 50 75 100
	Actual									
	Goal									25 50 75 100
	Actual									

Daily/Weekly Tasks	Date	Mon	Tue	Wed	Thur	Fri	Sat	Sun	Total	Achievement Bar
	Goal									25 50 75 100
	Actual									
	Goal									25 50 75 100
	Actual									
	Goal									25 50 75 100
	Actual									
	Goal									25 50 75 100
	Actual									

The 5-Minute Mindset

Step 4: Design a Plan
Step 5: Implement a Plan

Daily/Weekly Goal Tracker

Month_____

GOAL(S)

Daily/Weekly Tasks		Mon	Tue	Wed	Thur	Fri	Sat	Sun	Total	Achievement Bar
	Date									
	Goal									25 50 75 100
	Actual									
	Goal									25 50 75 100
	Actual									
	Goal									25 50 75 100
	Actual									
	Goal									25 50 75 100
	Actual									
	Goal									25 50 75 100
	Actual									

Daily/Weekly Tasks		Mon	Tue	Wed	Thur	Fri	Sat	Sun	Total	Achievement Bar
	Date									
	Goal									25 50 75 100
	Actual									
	Goal									25 50 75 100
	Actual									
	Goal									25 50 75 100
	Actual									
	Goal									25 50 75 100
	Actual									
	Goal									25 50 75 100
	Actual									

Daily/Weekly Tasks		Mon	Tue	Wed	Thur	Fri	Sat	Sun	Total	Achievement Bar
	Date									
	Goal									25 50 75 100
	Actual									
	Goal									25 50 75 100
	Actual									
	Goal									25 50 75 100
	Actual									
	Goal									25 50 75 100
	Actual									
	Goal									25 50 75 100
	Actual									

5-Minute Mindset

Step 4: Design a Plan
Step 5: Implement a Plan
Daily/Weekly Goal Tracker

Month_____

GOAL(S)

Daily/Weekly Tasks	Date	Mon	Tue	Wed	Thur	Fri	Sat	Sun	Total	Achievement Bar
	Goal									25 50 75 100
	Actual									
	Goal									25 50 75 100
	Actual									
	Goal									25 50 75 100
	Actual									
	Goal									25 50 75 100
	Actual									
	Goal									25 50 75 100
	Actual									

Daily/Weekly Tasks	Date	Mon	Tue	Wed	Thur	Fri	Sat	Sun	Total	Achievement Bar
	Goal									25 50 75 100
	Actual									
	Goal									25 50 75 100
	Actual									
	Goal									25 50 75 100
	Actual									
	Goal									25 50 75 100
	Actual									
	Goal									25 50 75 100
	Actual									

Daily/Weekly Tasks	Date	Mon	Tue	Wed	Thur	Fri	Sat	Sun	Total	Achievement Bar
	Goal									25 50 75 100
	Actual									
	Goal									25 50 75 100
	Actual									
	Goal									25 50 75 100
	Actual									
	Goal									25 50 75 100
	Actual									
	Goal									25 50 75 100
	Actual									

5-Minute Mindset (The)

Step 4: Design a Plan
Step 5: Implement a Plan
Daily/Weekly Goal Tracker

Month_____

GOAL(S)

Daily/Weekly Tasks	Date	Mon	Tue	Wed	Thur	Fri	Sat	Sun	Total	Achievement Bar
	Goal									25 50 75 100
	Actual									
	Goal									25 50 75 100
	Actual									
	Goal									25 50 75 100
	Actual									
	Goal									25 50 75 100
	Actual									
	Goal									25 50 75 100
	Actual									

Daily/Weekly Tasks	Date	Mon	Tue	Wed	Thur	Fri	Sat	Sun	Total	Achievement Bar
	Goal									25 50 75 100
	Actual									
	Goal									25 50 75 100
	Actual									
	Goal									25 50 75 100
	Actual									
	Goal									25 50 75 100
	Actual									
	Goal									25 50 75 100
	Actual									

Daily/Weekly Tasks	Date	Mon	Tue	Wed	Thur	Fri	Sat	Sun	Total	Achievement Bar
	Goal									25 50 75 100
	Actual									
	Goal									25 50 75 100
	Actual									
	Goal									25 50 75 100
	Actual									
	Goal									25 50 75 100
	Actual									
	Goal									25 50 75 100
	Actual									

5 The Minute Mindset

Step 4: Design a Plan
Step 5: Implement a Plan
Daily/Weekly Goal Tracker

Month_____

GOAL(S)

Daily/Weekly Tasks		Mon	Tue	Wed	Thur	Fri	Sat	Sun	Total	Achievement Bar
	Date									
	Goal									25 50 75 100
	Actual									
	Goal									25 50 75 100
	Actual									
	Goal									25 50 75 100
	Actual									
	Goal									25 50 75 100
	Actual									
	Goal									25 50 75 100
	Actual									

Daily/Weekly Tasks		Mon	Tue	Wed	Thur	Fri	Sat	Sun	Total	Achievement Bar
	Date									
	Goal									25 50 75 100
	Actual									
	Goal									25 50 75 100
	Actual									
	Goal									25 50 75 100
	Actual									
	Goal									25 50 75 100
	Actual									
	Goal									25 50 75 100
	Actual									

Daily/Weekly Tasks		Mon	Tue	Wed	Thur	Fri	Sat	Sun	Total	Achievement Bar
	Date									
	Goal									25 50 75 100
	Actual									
	Goal									25 50 75 100
	Actual									
	Goal									25 50 75 100
	Actual									
	Goal									25 50 75 100
	Actual									
	Goal									25 50 75 100
	Actual									

5-Minute Mindset The

Step 4: Design a Plan
Step 5: Implement a Plan   Month_____
Daily/Weekly Goal Tracker

GOAL(S)

Daily/Weekly Tasks		Mon	Tue	Wed	Thur	Fri	Sat	Sun	Total	Achievement Bar
	Date									
	Goal									25 50 75 100
	Actual									
	Goal									25 50 75 100
	Actual									
	Goal									25 50 75 100
	Actual									
	Goal									25 50 75 100
	Actual									
	Goal									25 50 75 100
	Actual									

Daily/Weekly Tasks		Mon	Tue	Wed	Thur	Fri	Sat	Sun	Total	Achievement Bar
	Date									
	Goal									25 50 75 100
	Actual									
	Goal									25 50 75 100
	Actual									
	Goal									25 50 75 100
	Actual									
	Goal									25 50 75 100
	Actual									
	Goal									25 50 75 100
	Actual									

Daily/Weekly Tasks		Mon	Tue	Wed	Thur	Fri	Sat	Sun	Total	Achievement Bar
	Date									
	Goal									25 50 75 100
	Actual									
	Goal									25 50 75 100
	Actual									
	Goal									25 50 75 100
	Actual									
	Goal									25 50 75 100
	Actual									
	Goal									25 50 75 100
	Actual									

5-Minute Mindset

Step 4: Design a Plan
Step 5: Implement a Plan
Daily/Weekly Goal Tracker

Month_____

GOAL(S)

Daily/Weekly Tasks	Date	Mon	Tue	Wed	Thur	Fri	Sat	Sun	Total	Achievement Bar
	Goal									25 50 75 100
	Actual									
	Goal									25 50 75 100
	Actual									
	Goal									25 50 75 100
	Actual									
	Goal									25 50 75 100
	Actual									
	Goal									25 50 75 100
	Actual									

Daily/Weekly Tasks	Date	Mon	Tue	Wed	Thur	Fri	Sat	Sun	Total	Achievement Bar
	Goal									25 50 75 100
	Actual									
	Goal									25 50 75 100
	Actual									
	Goal									25 50 75 100
	Actual									
	Goal									25 50 75 100
	Actual									
	Goal									25 50 75 100
	Actual									

Daily/Weekly Tasks	Date	Mon	Tue	Wed	Thur	Fri	Sat	Sun	Total	Achievement Bar
	Goal									25 50 75 100
	Actual									
	Goal									25 50 75 100
	Actual									
	Goal									25 50 75 100
	Actual									
	Goal									25 50 75 100
	Actual									
	Goal									25 50 75 100
	Actual									

The 5-Minute Mindset

Step 4: Design a Plan
Step 5: Implement a Plan

Month_____

Daily/Weekly Goal Tracker

GOAL(S)

Daily/Weekly Tasks		Mon	Tue	Wed	Thur	Fri	Sat	Sun	Total	Achievement Bar
	Date									
	Goal									25 50 75 100
	Actual									
	Goal									25 50 75 100
	Actual									
	Goal									25 50 75 100
	Actual									
	Goal									25 50 75 100
	Actual									
	Goal									25 50 75 100
	Actual									

Daily/Weekly Tasks		Mon	Tue	Wed	Thur	Fri	Sat	Sun	Total	Achievement Bar
	Date									
	Goal									25 50 75 100
	Actual									
	Goal									25 50 75 100
	Actual									
	Goal									25 50 75 100
	Actual									
	Goal									25 50 75 100
	Actual									
	Goal									25 50 75 100
	Actual									

Daily/Weekly Tasks		Mon	Tue	Wed	Thur	Fri	Sat	Sun	Total	Achievement Bar
	Date									
	Goal									25 50 75 100
	Actual									
	Goal									25 50 75 100
	Actual									
	Goal									25 50 75 100
	Actual									
	Goal									25 50 75 100
	Actual									
	Goal									25 50 75 100
	Actual									

5-Minute Mindset

Step 4: Design a Plan
Step 5: Implement a Plan
Daily/Weekly Goal Tracker

Month_____

GOAL(S)

Daily/Weekly Tasks	Date	Mon	Tue	Wed	Thur	Fri	Sat	Sun	Total	Achievement Bar
	Goal									25 50 75 100
	Actual									
	Goal									25 50 75 100
	Actual									
	Goal									25 50 75 100
	Actual									
	Goal									25 50 75 100
	Actual									
	Goal									25 50 75 100
	Actual									

Daily/Weekly Tasks	Date	Mon	Tue	Wed	Thur	Fri	Sat	Sun	Total	Achievement Bar
	Goal									25 50 75 100
	Actual									
	Goal									25 50 75 100
	Actual									
	Goal									25 50 75 100
	Actual									
	Goal									25 50 75 100
	Actual									
	Goal									25 50 75 100
	Actual									

Daily/Weekly Tasks	Date	Mon	Tue	Wed	Thur	Fri	Sat	Sun	Total	Achievement Bar
	Goal									25 50 75 100
	Actual									
	Goal									25 50 75 100
	Actual									
	Goal									25 50 75 100
	Actual									
	Goal									25 50 75 100
	Actual									
	Goal									25 50 75 100
	Actual									

The 5-Minute Mindset

Step 4: Design a Plan
Step 5: Implement a Plan   Month_____
Daily/Weekly Goal Tracker

GOAL(S)

Daily/Weekly Tasks		Mon	Tue	Wed	Thur	Fri	Sat	Sun	Total	Achievement Bar
	Date									
	Goal									25 50 75 100
	Actual									
	Goal									25 50 75 100
	Actual									
	Goal									25 50 75 100
	Actual									
	Goal									25 50 75 100
	Actual									
	Goal									25 50 75 100
	Actual									
Daily/Weekly Tasks		Mon	Tue	Wed	Thur	Fri	Sat	Sun	Total	Achievement Bar
	Date									
	Goal									25 50 75 100
	Actual									
	Goal									25 50 75 100
	Actual									
	Goal									25 50 75 100
	Actual									
	Goal									25 50 75 100
	Actual									
	Goal									25 50 75 100
	Actual									
Daily/Weekly Tasks		Mon	Tue	Wed	Thur	Fri	Sat	Sun	Total	Achievement Bar
	Date									
	Goal									25 50 75 100
	Actual									
	Goal									25 50 75 100
	Actual									
	Goal									25 50 75 100
	Actual									
	Goal									25 50 75 100
	Actual									
	Goal									25 50 75 100
	Actual									

5-Minute Mindset — The

Step 4: Design a Plan
Step 5: Implement a Plan
Daily/Weekly Goal Tracker

Month_____

GOAL(S)

Daily/Weekly Tasks		Mon	Tue	Wed	Thur	Fri	Sat	Sun	Total	Achievement Bar
	Date									
	Goal									25 50 75 100
	Actual									
	Goal									25 50 75 100
	Actual									
	Goal									25 50 75 100
	Actual									
	Goal									25 50 75 100
	Actual									
	Goal									25 50 75 100
	Actual									

Daily/Weekly Tasks		Mon	Tue	Wed	Thur	Fri	Sat	Sun	Total	Achievement Bar
	Date									
	Goal									25 50 75 100
	Actual									
	Goal									25 50 75 100
	Actual									
	Goal									25 50 75 100
	Actual									
	Goal									25 50 75 100
	Actual									
	Goal									25 50 75 100
	Actual									

Daily/Weekly Tasks		Mon	Tue	Wed	Thur	Fri	Sat	Sun	Total	Achievement Bar
	Date									
	Goal									25 50 75 100
	Actual									
	Goal									25 50 75 100
	Actual									
	Goal									25 50 75 100
	Actual									
	Goal									25 50 75 100
	Actual									
	Goal									25 50 75 100
	Actual									

The 5-Minute Mindset

Step 4: Design a Plan
Step 5: Implement a Plan

Month_____

Daily/Weekly Goal Tracker

GOAL(S)

Daily/Weekly Tasks		Mon	Tue	Wed	Thur	Fri	Sat	Sun	Total	Achievement Bar
	Date									
	Goal									25 50 75 100
	Actual									
	Goal									25 50 75 100
	Actual									
	Goal									25 50 75 100
	Actual									
	Goal									25 50 75 100
	Actual									
	Goal									25 50 75 100
	Actual									

Daily/Weekly Tasks		Mon	Tue	Wed	Thur	Fri	Sat	Sun	Total	Achievement Bar
	Date									
	Goal									25 50 75 100
	Actual									
	Goal									25 50 75 100
	Actual									
	Goal									25 50 75 100
	Actual									
	Goal									25 50 75 100
	Actual									
	Goal									25 50 75 100
	Actual									

Daily/Weekly Tasks		Mon	Tue	Wed	Thur	Fri	Sat	Sun	Total	Achievement Bar
	Date									
	Goal									25 50 75 100
	Actual									
	Goal									25 50 75 100
	Actual									
	Goal									25 50 75 100
	Actual									
	Goal									25 50 75 100
	Actual									
	Goal									25 50 75 100
	Actual									

5-Minute Mindset
The

Step 6: Provide Ongoing Motivation
Step 7: Interpret Results and Adjust Accordingly
Step 8: Celebrate Your Success
Step 9: Arrive at Your Destination

Date	Entries

The 5-Minute Mindset

Step 6: Provide Ongoing Motivation
Step 7: Interpret Results and Adjust Accordingly
Step 8: Celebrate Your Success
Step 9: Arrive at Your Destination

Date	Entries

The 5-Minute Mindset

Step 6: Provide Ongoing Motivation
Step 7: Interpret Results and Adjust Accordingly
Step 8: Celebrate Your Success
Step 9: Arrive at Your Destination

Date	Entries

The 5-Minute Mindset

Step 6: Provide Ongoing Motivation
Step 7: Interpret Results and Adjust Accordingly
Step 8: Celebrate Your Success
Step 9: Arrive at Your Destination

Date	Entries

The 5-Minute Mindset

Forms for # 4

(After you decide what area you want to work on, come back to this page and fill it in.)

_____

_____

_____

5-Minute Mindset — Step 1: Make A Decision

What area do you want to work on?
(Example: Spiritual, Physical, Social, Emotional, Educational, Financial)

5 **The** **-Minute** **Mindset**

Step 2: Write Your Story
and Find Your 'Whys'

What area in your life did you decide to work on?

**Make a list of your reasons for this decision or write stories
that illustrate why this decision is important to you.**

5-Minute Mindset

**Step 2: Write Your Story
and Find Your 'Whys'**

What area in your life did you decide to work on?

**Make a list of your reasons for this decision or write stories
that illustrate why this decision is important to you.**

The 5-Minute Mindset

Step 3: Set Goals
Long Term and Intermediate

Long Term Goal:	Deadline	Goal	Actual

Achievement Bar				
	25%	50%	75%	100%

Intermediate Goals or Tasks	Deadline	Goal	Actual	Achievement Bar
				25 50 75 100
				25 50 75 100
				25 50 75 100
				25 50 75 100
				25 50 75 100
				25 50 75 100
				25 50 75 100
				25 50 75 100
				25 50 75 100
				25 50 75 100
				25 50 75 100
				25 50 75 100
				25 50 75 100
				25 50 75 100
				25 50 75 100
				25 50 75 100
				25 50 75 100
				25 50 75 100

The 5-Minute Mindset

Step 4: Design a Plan
Brainstorm; Resources,
Principles, Rules and Guidelines

Goal / Due Date:

What resources of information are available to you? Do you know any experts? What are
the hard and fast rules that will lead to success? What are the core principles? What
guidelines are you going to set? How are you going to achieve your goal?

Priority	Entries

The 5-Minute Mindset

Step 4: Design a Plan
Step 5: Implement a Plan
Daily/Weekly Goal Tracker

Month_____

GOAL(S)

Daily/Weekly Tasks	Date	Mon	Tue	Wed	Thur	Fri	Sat	Sun	Total	Achievement Bar
	Goal									25 50 75 100
	Actual									
	Goal									25 50 75 100
	Actual									
	Goal									25 50 75 100
	Actual									
	Goal									25 50 75 100
	Actual									
	Goal									25 50 75 100
	Actual									

Daily/Weekly Tasks	Date	Mon	Tue	Wed	Thur	Fri	Sat	Sun	Total	Achievement Bar
	Goal									25 50 75 100
	Actual									
	Goal									25 50 75 100
	Actual									
	Goal									25 50 75 100
	Actual									
	Goal									25 50 75 100
	Actual									
	Goal									25 50 75 100
	Actual									

Daily/Weekly Tasks	Date	Mon	Tue	Wed	Thur	Fri	Sat	Sun	Total	Achievement Bar
	Goal									25 50 75 100
	Actual									
	Goal									25 50 75 100
	Actual									
	Goal									25 50 75 100
	Actual									
	Goal									25 50 75 100
	Actual									
	Goal									25 50 75 100
	Actual									

5-Minute Mindset The

Step 4: Design a Plan
Step 5: Implement a Plan

Month_____

Daily/Weekly Goal Tracker

GOAL(S)

Daily/Weekly Tasks		Mon	Tue	Wed	Thur	Fri	Sat	Sun	Total	Achievement Bar
	Date									
	Goal									25 50 75 100
	Actual									
	Goal									25 50 75 100
	Actual									
	Goal									25 50 75 100
	Actual									
	Goal									25 50 75 100
	Actual									
	Goal									25 50 75 100
	Actual									

Daily/Weekly Tasks		Mon	Tue	Wed	Thur	Fri	Sat	Sun	Total	Achievement Bar
	Date									
	Goal									25 50 75 100
	Actual									
	Goal									25 50 75 100
	Actual									
	Goal									25 50 75 100
	Actual									
	Goal									25 50 75 100
	Actual									
	Goal									25 50 75 100
	Actual									

Daily/Weekly Tasks		Mon	Tue	Wed	Thur	Fri	Sat	Sun	Total	Achievement Bar
	Date									
	Goal									25 50 75 100
	Actual									
	Goal									25 50 75 100
	Actual									
	Goal									25 50 75 100
	Actual									
	Goal									25 50 75 100
	Actual									
	Goal									25 50 75 100
	Actual									

The 5-Minute Mindset

Step 4: Design a Plan
Step 5: Implement a Plan
Daily/Weekly Goal Tracker

Month_____

GOAL(S)

Daily/Weekly Tasks		Mon	Tue	Wed	Thur	Fri	Sat	Sun	Total	Achievement Bar
	Date									
	Goal									25 50 75 100
	Actual									
	Goal									25 50 75 100
	Actual									
	Goal									25 50 75 100
	Actual									
	Goal									25 50 75 100
	Actual									
	Goal									25 50 75 100
	Actual									

Daily/Weekly Tasks		Mon	Tue	Wed	Thur	Fri	Sat	Sun	Total	Achievement Bar
	Date									
	Goal									25 50 75 100
	Actual									
	Goal									25 50 75 100
	Actual									
	Goal									25 50 75 100
	Actual									
	Goal									25 50 75 100
	Actual									
	Goal									25 50 75 100
	Actual									

Daily/Weekly Tasks		Mon	Tue	Wed	Thur	Fri	Sat	Sun	Total	Achievement Bar
	Date									
	Goal									25 50 75 100
	Actual									
	Goal									25 50 75 100
	Actual									
	Goal									25 50 75 100
	Actual									
	Goal									25 50 75 100
	Actual									
	Goal									25 50 75 100
	Actual									

5 The -Minute Mindset

Step 4: Design a Plan
Step 5: Implement a Plan
Daily/Weekly Goal Tracker

Month_____

GOAL(S)

Daily/Weekly Tasks		Mon	Tue	Wed	Thur	Fri	Sat	Sun	Total	Achievement Bar
	Date									
	Goal									25 50 75 100
	Actual									
	Goal									25 50 75 100
	Actual									
	Goal									25 50 75 100
	Actual									
	Goal									25 50 75 100
	Actual									
	Goal									25 50 75 100
	Actual									

Daily/Weekly Tasks		Mon	Tue	Wed	Thur	Fri	Sat	Sun	Total	Achievement Bar
	Date									
	Goal									25 50 75 100
	Actual									
	Goal									25 50 75 100
	Actual									
	Goal									25 50 75 100
	Actual									
	Goal									25 50 75 100
	Actual									
	Goal									25 50 75 100
	Actual									

Daily/Weekly Tasks		Mon	Tue	Wed	Thur	Fri	Sat	Sun	Total	Achievement Bar
	Date									
	Goal									25 50 75 100
	Actual									
	Goal									25 50 75 100
	Actual									
	Goal									25 50 75 100
	Actual									
	Goal									25 50 75 100
	Actual									
	Goal									25 50 75 100
	Actual									

5 The -Minute Mindset

Step 4: Design a Plan
Step 5: Implement a Plan
Daily/Weekly Goal Tracker

Month_____

GOAL(S)

Daily/Weekly Tasks	Date	Mon	Tue	Wed	Thur	Fri	Sat	Sun	Total	Achievement Bar
	Goal									25 50 75 100
	Actual									
	Goal									25 50 75 100
	Actual									
	Goal									25 50 75 100
	Actual									
	Goal									25 50 75 100
	Actual									
	Goal									25 50 75 100
	Actual									

Daily/Weekly Tasks	Date	Mon	Tue	Wed	Thur	Fri	Sat	Sun	Total	Achievement Bar
	Goal									25 50 75 100
	Actual									
	Goal									25 50 75 100
	Actual									
	Goal									25 50 75 100
	Actual									
	Goal									25 50 75 100
	Actual									
	Goal									25 50 75 100
	Actual									

Daily/Weekly Tasks	Date	Mon	Tue	Wed	Thur	Fri	Sat	Sun	Total	Achievement Bar
	Goal									25 50 75 100
	Actual									
	Goal									25 50 75 100
	Actual									
	Goal									25 50 75 100
	Actual									
	Goal									25 50 75 100
	Actual									
	Goal									25 50 75 100
	Actual									

The 5-Minute Mindset

Step 4: Design a Plan
Step 5: Implement a Plan

Daily/Weekly Goal Tracker

Month_____

GOAL(S)

Daily/Weekly Tasks		Mon	Tue	Wed	Thur	Fri	Sat	Sun	Total	Achievement Bar
	Date									
	Goal									25 50 75 100
	Actual									
	Goal									25 50 75 100
	Actual									
	Goal									25 50 75 100
	Actual									
	Goal									25 50 75 100
	Actual									
	Goal									25 50 75 100
	Actual									

Daily/Weekly Tasks		Mon	Tue	Wed	Thur	Fri	Sat	Sun	Total	Achievement Bar
	Date									
	Goal									25 50 75 100
	Actual									
	Goal									25 50 75 100
	Actual									
	Goal									25 50 75 100
	Actual									
	Goal									25 50 75 100
	Actual									
	Goal									25 50 75 100
	Actual									

Daily/Weekly Tasks		Mon	Tue	Wed	Thur	Fri	Sat	Sun	Total	Achievement Bar
	Date									
	Goal									25 50 75 100
	Actual									
	Goal									25 50 75 100
	Actual									
	Goal									25 50 75 100
	Actual									
	Goal									25 50 75 100
	Actual									
	Goal									25 50 75 100
	Actual									

The 5-Minute Mindset

Step 4: Design a Plan
Step 5: Implement a Plan

Daily/Weekly Goal Tracker

Month_____

GOAL(S)

Daily/Weekly Tasks		Mon	Tue	Wed	Thur	Fri	Sat	Sun	Total	Achievement Bar
	Date									
	Goal									25 50 75 100
	Actual									
	Goal									25 50 75 100
	Actual									
	Goal									25 50 75 100
	Actual									
	Goal									25 50 75 100
	Actual									
	Goal									25 50 75 100
	Actual									

Daily/Weekly Tasks		Mon	Tue	Wed	Thur	Fri	Sat	Sun	Total	Achievement Bar
	Date									
	Goal									25 50 75 100
	Actual									
	Goal									25 50 75 100
	Actual									
	Goal									25 50 75 100
	Actual									
	Goal									25 50 75 100
	Actual									
	Goal									25 50 75 100
	Actual									

Daily/Weekly Tasks		Mon	Tue	Wed	Thur	Fri	Sat	Sun	Total	Achievement Bar
	Date									
	Goal									25 50 75 100
	Actual									
	Goal									25 50 75 100
	Actual									
	Goal									25 50 75 100
	Actual									
	Goal									25 50 75 100
	Actual									
	Goal									25 50 75 100
	Actual									

Step 4: Design a Plan
Step 5: Implement a Plan   Month_____
Daily/Weekly Goal Tracker

The 5-Minute Mindset

GOAL(S)

Daily/Weekly Tasks		Mon	Tue	Wed	Thur	Fri	Sat	Sun	Total	Achievement Bar
	Date									
	Goal									25 50 75 100
	Actual									
	Goal									25 50 75 100
	Actual									
	Goal									25 50 75 100
	Actual									
	Goal									25 50 75 100
	Actual									
	Goal									25 50 75 100
	Actual									

Daily/Weekly Tasks		Mon	Tue	Wed	Thur	Fri	Sat	Sun	Total	Achievement Bar
	Date									
	Goal									25 50 75 100
	Actual									
	Goal									25 50 75 100
	Actual									
	Goal									25 50 75 100
	Actual									
	Goal									25 50 75 100
	Actual									
	Goal									25 50 75 100
	Actual									

Daily/Weekly Tasks		Mon	Tue	Wed	Thur	Fri	Sat	Sun	Total	Achievement Bar
	Date									
	Goal									25 50 75 100
	Actual									
	Goal									25 50 75 100
	Actual									
	Goal									25 50 75 100
	Actual									
	Goal									25 50 75 100
	Actual									
	Goal									25 50 75 100
	Actual									

The 5-Minute Mindset

Step 4: Design a Plan
Step 5: Implement a Plan
Daily/Weekly Goal Tracker

Month_____

GOAL(S)

Daily/Weekly Tasks		Mon	Tue	Wed	Thur	Fri	Sat	Sun	Total	Achievement Bar
	Date									
	Goal									25 50 75 100
	Actual									
	Goal									25 50 75 100
	Actual									
	Goal									25 50 75 100
	Actual									
	Goal									25 50 75 100
	Actual									
	Goal									25 50 75 100
	Actual									

Daily/Weekly Tasks		Mon	Tue	Wed	Thur	Fri	Sat	Sun	Total	Achievement Bar
	Date									
	Goal									25 50 75 100
	Actual									
	Goal									25 50 75 100
	Actual									
	Goal									25 50 75 100
	Actual									
	Goal									25 50 75 100
	Actual									
	Goal									25 50 75 100
	Actual									

Daily/Weekly Tasks		Mon	Tue	Wed	Thur	Fri	Sat	Sun	Total	Achievement Bar
	Date									
	Goal									25 50 75 100
	Actual									
	Goal									25 50 75 100
	Actual									
	Goal									25 50 75 100
	Actual									
	Goal									25 50 75 100
	Actual									
	Goal									25 50 75 100
	Actual									

The 5-Minute Mindset

Step 4: Design a Plan
Step 5: Implement a Plan
Daily/Weekly Goal Tracker

Month_____

GOAL(S)

Daily/Weekly Tasks		Mon	Tue	Wed	Thur	Fri	Sat	Sun	Total	Achievement Bar
	Date									
	Goal									25 50 75 100
	Actual									
	Goal									25 50 75 100
	Actual									
	Goal									25 50 75 100
	Actual									
	Goal									25 50 75 100
	Actual									
	Goal									25 50 75 100
	Actual									

Daily/Weekly Tasks		Mon	Tue	Wed	Thur	Fri	Sat	Sun	Total	Achievement Bar
	Date									
	Goal									25 50 75 100
	Actual									
	Goal									25 50 75 100
	Actual									
	Goal									25 50 75 100
	Actual									
	Goal									25 50 75 100
	Actual									
	Goal									25 50 75 100
	Actual									

Daily/Weekly Tasks		Mon	Tue	Wed	Thur	Fri	Sat	Sun	Total	Achievement Bar
	Date									
	Goal									25 50 75 100
	Actual									
	Goal									25 50 75 100
	Actual									
	Goal									25 50 75 100
	Actual									
	Goal									25 50 75 100
	Actual									
	Goal									25 50 75 100
	Actual									

The 5-Minute Mindset

Step 4: Design a Plan
Step 5: Implement a Plan
Daily/Weekly Goal Tracker

Month_____

GOAL(S)

Daily/Weekly Tasks		Mon	Tue	Wed	Thur	Fri	Sat	Sun	Total	Achievement Bar
	Date									
	Goal									25 50 75 100
	Actual									
	Goal									25 50 75 100
	Actual									
	Goal									25 50 75 100
	Actual									
	Goal									25 50 75 100
	Actual									
	Goal									25 50 75 100
	Actual									

Daily/Weekly Tasks		Mon	Tue	Wed	Thur	Fri	Sat	Sun	Total	Achievement Bar
	Date									
	Goal									25 50 75 100
	Actual									
	Goal									25 50 75 100
	Actual									
	Goal									25 50 75 100
	Actual									
	Goal									25 50 75 100
	Actual									
	Goal									25 50 75 100
	Actual									

Daily/Weekly Tasks		Mon	Tue	Wed	Thur	Fri	Sat	Sun	Total	Achievement Bar
	Date									
	Goal									25 50 75 100
	Actual									
	Goal									25 50 75 100
	Actual									
	Goal									25 50 75 100
	Actual									
	Goal									25 50 75 100
	Actual									
	Goal									25 50 75 100
	Actual									

5-Minute Mindset (The)

Step 4: Design a Plan
Step 5: Implement a Plan

Daily/Weekly Goal Tracker

Month_____

GOAL(S)

Daily/Weekly Tasks	Date	Mon	Tue	Wed	Thur	Fri	Sat	Sun	Total	Achievement Bar
	Goal									25 50 75 100
	Actual									
	Goal									25 50 75 100
	Actual									
	Goal									25 50 75 100
	Actual									
	Goal									25 50 75 100
	Actual									
	Goal									25 50 75 100
	Actual									

Daily/Weekly Tasks	Date	Mon	Tue	Wed	Thur	Fri	Sat	Sun	Total	Achievement Bar
	Goal									25 50 75 100
	Actual									
	Goal									25 50 75 100
	Actual									
	Goal									25 50 75 100
	Actual									
	Goal									25 50 75 100
	Actual									
	Goal									25 50 75 100
	Actual									

Daily/Weekly Tasks	Date	Mon	Tue	Wed	Thur	Fri	Sat	Sun	Total	Achievement Bar
	Goal									25 50 75 100
	Actual									
	Goal									25 50 75 100
	Actual									
	Goal									25 50 75 100
	Actual									
	Goal									25 50 75 100
	Actual									
	Goal									25 50 75 100
	Actual									

The 5-Minute Mindset

Step 4: Design a Plan
Step 5: Implement a Plan
Daily/Weekly Goal Tracker

Month_____

GOAL(S)

Daily/Weekly Tasks		Mon	Tue	Wed	Thur	Fri	Sat	Sun	Total	Achievement Bar
	Date									
	Goal									25 50 75 100
	Actual									
	Goal									25 50 75 100
	Actual									
	Goal									25 50 75 100
	Actual									
	Goal									25 50 75 100
	Actual									
	Goal									25 50 75 100
	Actual									

Daily/Weekly Tasks		Mon	Tue	Wed	Thur	Fri	Sat	Sun	Total	Achievement Bar
	Date									
	Goal									25 50 75 100
	Actual									
	Goal									25 50 75 100
	Actual									
	Goal									25 50 75 100
	Actual									
	Goal									25 50 75 100
	Actual									
	Goal									25 50 75 100
	Actual									

Daily/Weekly Tasks		Mon	Tue	Wed	Thur	Fri	Sat	Sun	Total	Achievement Bar
	Date									
	Goal									25 50 75 100
	Actual									
	Goal									25 50 75 100
	Actual									
	Goal									25 50 75 100
	Actual									
	Goal									25 50 75 100
	Actual									
	Goal									25 50 75 100
	Actual									

5-Minute Mindset

Step 4: Design a Plan
Step 5: Implement a Plan

Daily/Weekly Goal Tracker

Month_____

GOAL(S)

Daily/Weekly Tasks		Mon	Tue	Wed	Thur	Fri	Sat	Sun	Total	Achievement Bar
	Date									
	Goal									25 50 75 100
	Actual									
	Goal									25 50 75 100
	Actual									
	Goal									25 50 75 100
	Actual									
	Goal									25 50 75 100
	Actual									
	Goal									25 50 75 100
	Actual									

Daily/Weekly Tasks		Mon	Tue	Wed	Thur	Fri	Sat	Sun	Total	Achievement Bar
	Date									
	Goal									25 50 75 100
	Actual									
	Goal									25 50 75 100
	Actual									
	Goal									25 50 75 100
	Actual									
	Goal									25 50 75 100
	Actual									
	Goal									25 50 75 100
	Actual									

Daily/Weekly Tasks		Mon	Tue	Wed	Thur	Fri	Sat	Sun	Total	Achievement Bar
	Date									
	Goal									25 50 75 100
	Actual									
	Goal									25 50 75 100
	Actual									
	Goal									25 50 75 100
	Actual									
	Goal									25 50 75 100
	Actual									
	Goal									25 50 75 100
	Actual									

The 5-Minute Mindset

Step 4: Design a Plan
Step 5: Implement a Plan
Daily/Weekly Goal Tracker

Month_____

GOAL(S)

Daily/Weekly Tasks		Mon	Tue	Wed	Thur	Fri	Sat	Sun	Total	Achievement Bar
	Date									
	Goal									25 50 75 100
	Actual									
	Goal									25 50 75 100
	Actual									
	Goal									25 50 75 100
	Actual									
	Goal									25 50 75 100
	Actual									
	Goal									25 50 75 100
	Actual									

Daily/Weekly Tasks		Mon	Tue	Wed	Thur	Fri	Sat	Sun	Total	Achievement Bar
	Date									
	Goal									25 50 75 100
	Actual									
	Goal									25 50 75 100
	Actual									
	Goal									25 50 75 100
	Actual									
	Goal									25 50 75 100
	Actual									
	Goal									25 50 75 100
	Actual									

Daily/Weekly Tasks		Mon	Tue	Wed	Thur	Fri	Sat	Sun	Total	Achievement Bar
	Date									
	Goal									25 50 75 100
	Actual									
	Goal									25 50 75 100
	Actual									
	Goal									25 50 75 100
	Actual									
	Goal									25 50 75 100
	Actual									
	Goal									25 50 75 100
	Actual									

5-Minute Mindset The

Step 4: Design a Plan
Step 5: Implement a Plan

Daily/Weekly Goal Tracker

Month_____

GOAL(S)

Daily/Weekly Tasks	Date	Mon	Tue	Wed	Thur	Fri	Sat	Sun	Total	Achievement Bar
	Goal									25 50 75 100
	Actual									
	Goal									25 50 75 100
	Actual									
	Goal									25 50 75 100
	Actual									
	Goal									25 50 75 100
	Actual									
	Goal									25 50 75 100
	Actual									

Daily/Weekly Tasks	Date	Mon	Tue	Wed	Thur	Fri	Sat	Sun	Total	Achievement Bar
	Goal									25 50 75 100
	Actual									
	Goal									25 50 75 100
	Actual									
	Goal									25 50 75 100
	Actual									
	Goal									25 50 75 100
	Actual									
	Goal									25 50 75 100
	Actual									

Daily/Weekly Tasks	Date	Mon	Tue	Wed	Thur	Fri	Sat	Sun	Total	Achievement Bar
	Goal									25 50 75 100
	Actual									
	Goal									25 50 75 100
	Actual									
	Goal									25 50 75 100
	Actual									
	Goal									25 50 75 100
	Actual									
	Goal									25 50 75 100
	Actual									

			Step 4: Design a Plan							

The 5-Minute Mindset

Step 4: Design a Plan
Step 5: Implement a Plan
Daily/Weekly Goal Tracker

Month_____

GOAL(S)

Daily/Weekly Tasks		Mon	Tue	Wed	Thur	Fri	Sat	Sun	Total	Achievement Bar
	Date									
	Goal									25 50 75 100
	Actual									
	Goal									25 50 75 100
	Actual									
	Goal									25 50 75 100
	Actual									
	Goal									25 50 75 100
	Actual									
	Goal									25 50 75 100
	Actual									

Daily/Weekly Tasks		Mon	Tue	Wed	Thur	Fri	Sat	Sun	Total	Achievement Bar
	Date									
	Goal									25 50 75 100
	Actual									
	Goal									25 50 75 100
	Actual									
	Goal									25 50 75 100
	Actual									
	Goal									25 50 75 100
	Actual									
	Goal									25 50 75 100
	Actual									

Daily/Weekly Tasks		Mon	Tue	Wed	Thur	Fri	Sat	Sun	Total	Achievement Bar
	Date									
	Goal									25 50 75 100
	Actual									
	Goal									25 50 75 100
	Actual									
	Goal									25 50 75 100
	Actual									
	Goal									25 50 75 100
	Actual									
	Goal									25 50 75 100
	Actual									

5-Minute Mindset

Step 4: Design a Plan
Step 5: Implement a Plan
Daily/Weekly Goal Tracker

Month_____

GOAL(S)

Daily/Weekly Tasks		Mon	Tue	Wed	Thur	Fri	Sat	Sun	Total	Achievement Bar
	Date									
	Goal									25 50 75 100
	Actual									
	Goal									25 50 75 100
	Actual									
	Goal									25 50 75 100
	Actual									
	Goal									25 50 75 100
	Actual									
	Goal									25 50 75 100
	Actual									

Daily/Weekly Tasks		Mon	Tue	Wed	Thur	Fri	Sat	Sun	Total	Achievement Bar
	Date									
	Goal									25 50 75 100
	Actual									
	Goal									25 50 75 100
	Actual									
	Goal									25 50 75 100
	Actual									
	Goal									25 50 75 100
	Actual									
	Goal									25 50 75 100
	Actual									

Daily/Weekly Tasks		Mon	Tue	Wed	Thur	Fri	Sat	Sun	Total	Achievement Bar
	Date									
	Goal									25 50 75 100
	Actual									
	Goal									25 50 75 100
	Actual									
	Goal									25 50 75 100
	Actual									
	Goal									25 50 75 100
	Actual									
	Goal									25 50 75 100
	Actual									

5-Minute Mindset

Step 6: Provide Ongoing Motivation
Step 7: Interpret Results and Adjust Accordingly
Step 8: Celebrate Your Success
Step 9: Arrive at Your Destination

Date	Entries

5-Minute Mindset

Step 6: Provide Ongoing Motivation
Step 7: Interpret Results and Adjust Accordingly
Step 8: Celebrate Your Success
Step 9: Arrive at Your Destination

Date	Entries

The 5-Minute Mindset

Step 6: Provide Ongoing Motivation
Step 7: Interpret Results and Adjust Accordingly
Step 8: Celebrate Your Success
Step 9: Arrive at Your Destination

Date	Entries

	Step 6: Provide Ongoing Motivation
The 5-Minute Mindset	Step 7: Interpret Results and Adjust Accordingly
	Step 8: Celebrate Your Success
	Step 9: Arrive at Your Destination

Date	Entries

The 5-Minute Mindset

Forms for # 5

**(After you decide what area you want to work
on, come back to this page and fill it in.)**

_____

_____

_____

5-Minute Mindset

Step 1: Make A Decision

What area do you want to work on?
(Example: Spiritual, Physical, Social, Emotional, Educational, Financial)

The 5-Minute Mindset

Step 2: Write Your Story
and Find Your 'Whys'

What area in your life did you decide to work on?

**Make a list of your reasons for this decision or write stories
that illustrate why this decision is important to you.**

The 5-Minute Mindset

Step 2: Write Your Story and Find Your 'Whys'

What area in your life did you decide to work on?

Make a list of your reasons for this decision or write stories that illustrate why this decision is important to you.

The 5-Minute Mindset

Step 3: Set Goals
Long Term and Intermediate

Long Term Goal:	Deadline	Goal	Actual

Achievement Bar			
25%	50%	75%	100%

Intermediate Goals or Tasks	Deadline	Goal	Actual	Achievement Bar
				25 50 75 100
				25 50 75 100
				25 50 75 100
				25 50 75 100
				25 50 75 100
				25 50 75 100
				25 50 75 100
				25 50 75 100
				25 50 75 100
				25 50 75 100
				25 50 75 100
				25 50 75 100
				25 50 75 100
				25 50 75 100
				25 50 75 100
				25 50 75 100
				25 50 75 100
				25 50 75 100

The 5-Minute Mindset

Step 4: Design a Plan
Brainstorm; Resources,
Principles, Rules and Guidelines

Goal / Due Date:

What resources of information are available to you? Do you know any experts? What are the hard and fast rules that will lead to success? What are the core principles? What guidelines are you going to set? How are you going to achieve your goal?

Priority	Entries

The 5-Minute Mindset

Step 4: Design a Plan
Step 5: Implement a Plan
Daily/Weekly Goal Tracker

Month_____

GOAL(S)

Daily/Weekly Tasks		Mon	Tue	Wed	Thur	Fri	Sat	Sun	Total	Achievement Bar
	Date									
	Goal									25 50 75 100
	Actual									
	Goal									25 50 75 100
	Actual									
	Goal									25 50 75 100
	Actual									
	Goal									25 50 75 100
	Actual									
	Goal									25 50 75 100
	Actual									

Daily/Weekly Tasks		Mon	Tue	Wed	Thur	Fri	Sat	Sun	Total	Achievement Bar
	Date									
	Goal									25 50 75 100
	Actual									
	Goal									25 50 75 100
	Actual									
	Goal									25 50 75 100
	Actual									
	Goal									25 50 75 100
	Actual									
	Goal									25 50 75 100
	Actual									

Daily/Weekly Tasks		Mon	Tue	Wed	Thur	Fri	Sat	Sun	Total	Achievement Bar
	Date									
	Goal									25 50 75 100
	Actual									
	Goal									25 50 75 100
	Actual									
	Goal									25 50 75 100
	Actual									
	Goal									25 50 75 100
	Actual									
	Goal									25 50 75 100
	Actual									

5 The -Minute Mindset

Step 4: Design a Plan
Step 5: Implement a Plan
Daily/Weekly Goal Tracker

Month_____

GOAL(S)

Daily/Weekly Tasks	Date	Mon	Tue	Wed	Thur	Fri	Sat	Sun	Total	Achievement Bar
	Goal									25 50 75 100
	Actual									
	Goal									25 50 75 100
	Actual									
	Goal									25 50 75 100
	Actual									
	Goal									25 50 75 100
	Actual									
	Goal									25 50 75 100
	Actual									

Daily/Weekly Tasks	Date	Mon	Tue	Wed	Thur	Fri	Sat	Sun	Total	Achievement Bar
	Goal									25 50 75 100
	Actual									
	Goal									25 50 75 100
	Actual									
	Goal									25 50 75 100
	Actual									
	Goal									25 50 75 100
	Actual									
	Goal									25 50 75 100
	Actual									

Daily/Weekly Tasks	Date	Mon	Tue	Wed	Thur	Fri	Sat	Sun	Total	Achievement Bar
	Goal									25 50 75 100
	Actual									
	Goal									25 50 75 100
	Actual									
	Goal									25 50 75 100
	Actual									
	Goal									25 50 75 100
	Actual									
	Goal									25 50 75 100
	Actual									

5-Minute Mindset

Step 4: Design a Plan
Step 5: Implement a Plan   Month_____

Daily/Weekly Goal Tracker

GOAL(S)

Daily/Weekly Tasks		Mon	Tue	Wed	Thur	Fri	Sat	Sun	Total	Achievement Bar
	Date									
	Goal									25 50 75 100
	Actual									
	Goal									25 50 75 100
	Actual									
	Goal									25 50 75 100
	Actual									
	Goal									25 50 75 100
	Actual									
	Goal									25 50 75 100
	Actual									

Daily/Weekly Tasks		Mon	Tue	Wed	Thur	Fri	Sat	Sun	Total	Achievement Bar
	Date									
	Goal									25 50 75 100
	Actual									
	Goal									25 50 75 100
	Actual									
	Goal									25 50 75 100
	Actual									
	Goal									25 50 75 100
	Actual									
	Goal									25 50 75 100
	Actual									

Daily/Weekly Tasks		Mon	Tue	Wed	Thur	Fri	Sat	Sun	Total	Achievement Bar
	Date									
	Goal									25 50 75 100
	Actual									
	Goal									25 50 75 100
	Actual									
	Goal									25 50 75 100
	Actual									
	Goal									25 50 75 100
	Actual									
	Goal									25 50 75 100
	Actual									

5-Minute Mindset

Step 4: Design a Plan
Step 5: Implement a Plan
Daily/Weekly Goal Tracker

Month_____

GOAL(S)

Daily/Weekly Tasks	Date	Mon	Tue	Wed	Thur	Fri	Sat	Sun	Total	Achievement Bar
	Goal									25 50 75 100
	Actual									
	Goal									25 50 75 100
	Actual									
	Goal									25 50 75 100
	Actual									
	Goal									25 50 75 100
	Actual									
	Goal									25 50 75 100
	Actual									

Daily/Weekly Tasks	Date	Mon	Tue	Wed	Thur	Fri	Sat	Sun	Total	Achievement Bar
	Goal									25 50 75 100
	Actual									
	Goal									25 50 75 100
	Actual									
	Goal									25 50 75 100
	Actual									
	Goal									25 50 75 100
	Actual									
	Goal									25 50 75 100
	Actual									

Daily/Weekly Tasks	Date	Mon	Tue	Wed	Thur	Fri	Sat	Sun	Total	Achievement Bar
	Goal									25 50 75 100
	Actual									
	Goal									25 50 75 100
	Actual									
	Goal									25 50 75 100
	Actual									
	Goal									25 50 75 100
	Actual									
	Goal									25 50 75 100
	Actual									

The 5-Minute Mindset

Step 4: Design a Plan
Step 5: Implement a Plan
Daily/Weekly Goal Tracker

Month_____

GOAL(S)

Daily/Weekly Tasks		Mon	Tue	Wed	Thur	Fri	Sat	Sun	Total	Achievement Bar
	Date									
	Goal									25 50 75 100
	Actual									
	Goal									25 50 75 100
	Actual									
	Goal									25 50 75 100
	Actual									
	Goal									25 50 75 100
	Actual									
	Goal									25 50 75 100
	Actual									

Daily/Weekly Tasks		Mon	Tue	Wed	Thur	Fri	Sat	Sun	Total	Achievement Bar
	Date									
	Goal									25 50 75 100
	Actual									
	Goal									25 50 75 100
	Actual									
	Goal									25 50 75 100
	Actual									
	Goal									25 50 75 100
	Actual									
	Goal									25 50 75 100
	Actual									

Daily/Weekly Tasks		Mon	Tue	Wed	Thur	Fri	Sat	Sun	Total	Achievement Bar
	Date									
	Goal									25 50 75 100
	Actual									
	Goal									25 50 75 100
	Actual									
	Goal									25 50 75 100
	Actual									
	Goal									25 50 75 100
	Actual									
	Goal									25 50 75 100
	Actual									

5-Minute Mindset (The)

Step 4: Design a Plan
Step 5: Implement a Plan   Month_____
Daily/Weekly Goal Tracker

GOAL(S)

Daily/Weekly Tasks		Mon	Tue	Wed	Thur	Fri	Sat	Sun	Total	Achievement Bar
	Date									
	Goal									25 50 75 100
	Actual									
	Goal									25 50 75 100
	Actual									
	Goal									25 50 75 100
	Actual									
	Goal									25 50 75 100
	Actual									
	Goal									25 50 75 100
	Actual									

Daily/Weekly Tasks		Mon	Tue	Wed	Thur	Fri	Sat	Sun	Total	Achievement Bar
	Date									
	Goal									25 50 75 100
	Actual									
	Goal									25 50 75 100
	Actual									
	Goal									25 50 75 100
	Actual									
	Goal									25 50 75 100
	Actual									
	Goal									25 50 75 100
	Actual									

Daily/Weekly Tasks		Mon	Tue	Wed	Thur	Fri	Sat	Sun	Total	Achievement Bar
	Date									
	Goal									25 50 75 100
	Actual									
	Goal									25 50 75 100
	Actual									
	Goal									25 50 75 100
	Actual									
	Goal									25 50 75 100
	Actual									
	Goal									25 50 75 100
	Actual									

The 5-Minute Mindset

Step 4: Design a Plan
Step 5: Implement a Plan   Month_____

Daily/Weekly Goal Tracker

GOAL(S)

Daily/Weekly Tasks		Mon	Tue	Wed	Thur	Fri	Sat	Sun	Total	Achievement Bar
	Date									
	Goal									25 50 75 100
	Actual									
	Goal									25 50 75 100
	Actual									
	Goal									25 50 75 100
	Actual									
	Goal									25 50 75 100
	Actual									
	Goal									25 50 75 100
	Actual									

Daily/Weekly Tasks		Mon	Tue	Wed	Thur	Fri	Sat	Sun	Total	Achievement Bar
	Date									
	Goal									25 50 75 100
	Actual									
	Goal									25 50 75 100
	Actual									
	Goal									25 50 75 100
	Actual									
	Goal									25 50 75 100
	Actual									
	Goal									25 50 75 100
	Actual									

Daily/Weekly Tasks		Mon	Tue	Wed	Thur	Fri	Sat	Sun	Total	Achievement Bar
	Date									
	Goal									25 50 75 100
	Actual									
	Goal									25 50 75 100
	Actual									
	Goal									25 50 75 100
	Actual									
	Goal									25 50 75 100
	Actual									
	Goal									25 50 75 100
	Actual									

The 5-Minute Mindset

Step 4: Design a Plan
Step 5: Implement a Plan

Daily/Weekly Goal Tracker

Month_____

GOAL(S)

Daily/Weekly Tasks		Mon	Tue	Wed	Thur	Fri	Sat	Sun	Total	Achievement Bar
	Date									
	Goal									25 50 75 100
	Actual									
	Goal									25 50 75 100
	Actual									
	Goal									25 50 75 100
	Actual									
	Goal									25 50 75 100
	Actual									
	Goal									25 50 75 100
	Actual									

Daily/Weekly Tasks		Mon	Tue	Wed	Thur	Fri	Sat	Sun	Total	Achievement Bar
	Date									
	Goal									25 50 75 100
	Actual									
	Goal									25 50 75 100
	Actual									
	Goal									25 50 75 100
	Actual									
	Goal									25 50 75 100
	Actual									
	Goal									25 50 75 100
	Actual									

Daily/Weekly Tasks		Mon	Tue	Wed	Thur	Fri	Sat	Sun	Total	Achievement Bar
	Date									
	Goal									25 50 75 100
	Actual									
	Goal									25 50 75 100
	Actual									
	Goal									25 50 75 100
	Actual									
	Goal									25 50 75 100
	Actual									
	Goal									25 50 75 100
	Actual									

5-Minute Mindset

Step 4: Design a Plan
Step 5: Implement a Plan

Month_____

Daily/Weekly Goal Tracker

GOAL(S)

Daily/Weekly Tasks		Mon	Tue	Wed	Thur	Fri	Sat	Sun	Total	Achievement Bar
	Date									
	Goal									25 50 75 100
	Actual									
	Goal									25 50 75 100
	Actual									
	Goal									25 50 75 100
	Actual									
	Goal									25 50 75 100
	Actual									
	Goal									25 50 75 100
	Actual									

Daily/Weekly Tasks		Mon	Tue	Wed	Thur	Fri	Sat	Sun	Total	Achievement Bar
	Date									
	Goal									25 50 75 100
	Actual									
	Goal									25 50 75 100
	Actual									
	Goal									25 50 75 100
	Actual									
	Goal									25 50 75 100
	Actual									
	Goal									25 50 75 100
	Actual									

Daily/Weekly Tasks		Mon	Tue	Wed	Thur	Fri	Sat	Sun	Total	Achievement Bar
	Date									
	Goal									25 50 75 100
	Actual									
	Goal									25 50 75 100
	Actual									
	Goal									25 50 75 100
	Actual									
	Goal									25 50 75 100
	Actual									
	Goal									25 50 75 100
	Actual									

The 5-Minute Mindset

Step 4: Design a Plan
Step 5: Implement a Plan
Daily/Weekly Goal Tracker

Month_____

GOAL(S)

Daily/Weekly Tasks		Mon	Tue	Wed	Thur	Fri	Sat	Sun	Total	Achievement Bar
	Date									
	Goal									25 50 75 100
	Actual									
	Goal									25 50 75 100
	Actual									
	Goal									25 50 75 100
	Actual									
	Goal									25 50 75 100
	Actual									
	Goal									25 50 75 100
	Actual									

Daily/Weekly Tasks		Mon	Tue	Wed	Thur	Fri	Sat	Sun	Total	Achievement Bar
	Date									
	Goal									25 50 75 100
	Actual									
	Goal									25 50 75 100
	Actual									
	Goal									25 50 75 100
	Actual									
	Goal									25 50 75 100
	Actual									
	Goal									25 50 75 100
	Actual									

Daily/Weekly Tasks		Mon	Tue	Wed	Thur	Fri	Sat	Sun	Total	Achievement Bar
	Date									
	Goal									25 50 75 100
	Actual									
	Goal									25 50 75 100
	Actual									
	Goal									25 50 75 100
	Actual									
	Goal									25 50 75 100
	Actual									
	Goal									25 50 75 100
	Actual									

5-Minute Mindset (logo)

Step 4: Design a Plan
Step 5: Implement a Plan
Daily/Weekly Goal Tracker

Month_____

GOAL(S)

Daily/Weekly Tasks		Mon	Tue	Wed	Thur	Fri	Sat	Sun	Total	Achievement Bar
	Date									
	Goal									25 50 75 100
	Actual									
	Goal									25 50 75 100
	Actual									
	Goal									25 50 75 100
	Actual									
	Goal									25 50 75 100
	Actual									
	Goal									25 50 75 100
	Actual									

Daily/Weekly Tasks		Mon	Tue	Wed	Thur	Fri	Sat	Sun	Total	Achievement Bar
	Date									
	Goal									25 50 75 100
	Actual									
	Goal									25 50 75 100
	Actual									
	Goal									25 50 75 100
	Actual									
	Goal									25 50 75 100
	Actual									
	Goal									25 50 75 100
	Actual									

Daily/Weekly Tasks		Mon	Tue	Wed	Thur	Fri	Sat	Sun	Total	Achievement Bar
	Date									
	Goal									25 50 75 100
	Actual									
	Goal									25 50 75 100
	Actual									
	Goal									25 50 75 100
	Actual									
	Goal									25 50 75 100
	Actual									
	Goal									25 50 75 100
	Actual									

5-Minute Mindset

Step 4: Design a Plan
Step 5: Implement a Plan
Daily/Weekly Goal Tracker

Month_____

GOAL(S)

Daily/Weekly Tasks		Mon	Tue	Wed	Thur	Fri	Sat	Sun	Total	Achievement Bar
	Date									
	Goal									25 50 75 100
	Actual									
	Goal									25 50 75 100
	Actual									
	Goal									25 50 75 100
	Actual									
	Goal									25 50 75 100
	Actual									
	Goal									25 50 75 100
	Actual									

Daily/Weekly Tasks		Mon	Tue	Wed	Thur	Fri	Sat	Sun	Total	Achievement Bar
	Date									
	Goal									25 50 75 100
	Actual									
	Goal									25 50 75 100
	Actual									
	Goal									25 50 75 100
	Actual									
	Goal									25 50 75 100
	Actual									
	Goal									25 50 75 100
	Actual									

Daily/Weekly Tasks		Mon	Tue	Wed	Thur	Fri	Sat	Sun	Total	Achievement Bar
	Date									
	Goal									25 50 75 100
	Actual									
	Goal									25 50 75 100
	Actual									
	Goal									25 50 75 100
	Actual									
	Goal									25 50 75 100
	Actual									
	Goal									25 50 75 100
	Actual									

5-Minute Mindset

Step 4: Design a Plan
Step 5: Implement a Plan

Daily/Weekly Goal Tracker

Month_____

GOAL(S)

Daily/Weekly Tasks	Date	Mon	Tue	Wed	Thur	Fri	Sat	Sun	Total	Achievement Bar
	Goal									25 50 75 100
	Actual									
	Goal									25 50 75 100
	Actual									
	Goal									25 50 75 100
	Actual									
	Goal									25 50 75 100
	Actual									
	Goal									25 50 75 100
	Actual									

Daily/Weekly Tasks	Date	Mon	Tue	Wed	Thur	Fri	Sat	Sun	Total	Achievement Bar
	Goal									25 50 75 100
	Actual									
	Goal									25 50 75 100
	Actual									
	Goal									25 50 75 100
	Actual									
	Goal									25 50 75 100
	Actual									
	Goal									25 50 75 100
	Actual									

Daily/Weekly Tasks	Date	Mon	Tue	Wed	Thur	Fri	Sat	Sun	Total	Achievement Bar
	Goal									25 50 75 100
	Actual									
	Goal									25 50 75 100
	Actual									
	Goal									25 50 75 100
	Actual									
	Goal									25 50 75 100
	Actual									
	Goal									25 50 75 100
	Actual									

The 5-Minute Mindset

Step 4: Design a Plan
Step 5: Implement a Plan

Daily/Weekly Goal Tracker

Month_____

GOAL(S)

Daily/Weekly Tasks		Mon	Tue	Wed	Thur	Fri	Sat	Sun	Total	Achievement Bar
	Date									
	Goal									25 50 75 100
	Actual									
	Goal									25 50 75 100
	Actual									
	Goal									25 50 75 100
	Actual									
	Goal									25 50 75 100
	Actual									
	Goal									25 50 75 100
	Actual									

Daily/Weekly Tasks		Mon	Tue	Wed	Thur	Fri	Sat	Sun	Total	Achievement Bar
	Date									
	Goal									25 50 75 100
	Actual									
	Goal									25 50 75 100
	Actual									
	Goal									25 50 75 100
	Actual									
	Goal									25 50 75 100
	Actual									
	Goal									25 50 75 100
	Actual									

Daily/Weekly Tasks		Mon	Tue	Wed	Thur	Fri	Sat	Sun	Total	Achievement Bar
	Date									
	Goal									25 50 75 100
	Actual									
	Goal									25 50 75 100
	Actual									
	Goal									25 50 75 100
	Actual									
	Goal									25 50 75 100
	Actual									
	Goal									25 50 75 100
	Actual									

5-Minute Mindset

Step 4: Design a Plan
Step 5: Implement a Plan
Daily/Weekly Goal Tracker

Month_____

GOAL(S)

Daily/Weekly Tasks		Mon	Tue	Wed	Thur	Fri	Sat	Sun	Total	Achievement Bar
	Date									
	Goal									25 50 75 100
	Actual									
	Goal									25 50 75 100
	Actual									
	Goal									25 50 75 100
	Actual									
	Goal									25 50 75 100
	Actual									
	Goal									25 50 75 100
	Actual									

Daily/Weekly Tasks		Mon	Tue	Wed	Thur	Fri	Sat	Sun	Total	Achievement Bar
	Date									
	Goal									25 50 75 100
	Actual									
	Goal									25 50 75 100
	Actual									
	Goal									25 50 75 100
	Actual									
	Goal									25 50 75 100
	Actual									
	Goal									25 50 75 100
	Actual									

Daily/Weekly Tasks		Mon	Tue	Wed	Thur	Fri	Sat	Sun	Total	Achievement Bar
	Date									
	Goal									25 50 75 100
	Actual									
	Goal									25 50 75 100
	Actual									
	Goal									25 50 75 100
	Actual									
	Goal									25 50 75 100
	Actual									

The 5-Minute Mindset

Step 4: Design a Plan
Step 5: Implement a Plan

Daily/Weekly Goal Tracker

Month_____

GOAL(S)

Daily/Weekly Tasks		Mon	Tue	Wed	Thur	Fri	Sat	Sun	Total	Achievement Bar
	Date									
	Goal									25 50 75 100
	Actual									
	Goal									25 50 75 100
	Actual									
	Goal									25 50 75 100
	Actual									
	Goal									25 50 75 100
	Actual									
	Goal									25 50 75 100
	Actual									

Daily/Weekly Tasks		Mon	Tue	Wed	Thur	Fri	Sat	Sun	Total	Achievement Bar
	Date									
	Goal									25 50 75 100
	Actual									
	Goal									25 50 75 100
	Actual									
	Goal									25 50 75 100
	Actual									
	Goal									25 50 75 100
	Actual									
	Goal									25 50 75 100
	Actual									

Daily/Weekly Tasks		Mon	Tue	Wed	Thur	Fri	Sat	Sun	Total	Achievement Bar
	Date									
	Goal									25 50 75 100
	Actual									
	Goal									25 50 75 100
	Actual									
	Goal									25 50 75 100
	Actual									
	Goal									25 50 75 100
	Actual									
	Goal									25 50 75 100
	Actual									

The 5-Minute Mindset

Step 4: Design a Plan
Step 5: Implement a Plan
Daily/Weekly Goal Tracker

Month_____

GOAL(S)

Daily/Weekly Tasks	Date	Mon	Tue	Wed	Thur	Fri	Sat	Sun	Total	Achievement Bar
	Goal									25 50 75 100
	Actual									
	Goal									25 50 75 100
	Actual									
	Goal									25 50 75 100
	Actual									
	Goal									25 50 75 100
	Actual									
	Goal									25 50 75 100
	Actual									

Daily/Weekly Tasks	Date	Mon	Tue	Wed	Thur	Fri	Sat	Sun	Total	Achievement Bar
	Goal									25 50 75 100
	Actual									
	Goal									25 50 75 100
	Actual									
	Goal									25 50 75 100
	Actual									
	Goal									25 50 75 100
	Actual									
	Goal									25 50 75 100
	Actual									

Daily/Weekly Tasks	Date	Mon	Tue	Wed	Thur	Fri	Sat	Sun	Total	Achievement Bar
	Goal									25 50 75 100
	Actual									
	Goal									25 50 75 100
	Actual									
	Goal									25 50 75 100
	Actual									
	Goal									25 50 75 100
	Actual									
	Goal									25 50 75 100
	Actual									

The 5-Minute Mindset

Step 4: Design a Plan
Step 5: Implement a Plan
Daily/Weekly Goal Tracker

Month_____

GOAL(S)

Daily/Weekly Tasks		Mon	Tue	Wed	Thur	Fri	Sat	Sun	Total	Achievement Bar
	Date									
	Goal									25 50 75 100
	Actual									
	Goal									25 50 75 100
	Actual									
	Goal									25 50 75 100
	Actual									
	Goal									25 50 75 100
	Actual									
	Goal									25 50 75 100
	Actual									

Daily/Weekly Tasks		Mon	Tue	Wed	Thur	Fri	Sat	Sun	Total	Achievement Bar
	Date									
	Goal									25 50 75 100
	Actual									
	Goal									25 50 75 100
	Actual									
	Goal									25 50 75 100
	Actual									
	Goal									25 50 75 100
	Actual									
	Goal									25 50 75 100
	Actual									

Daily/Weekly Tasks		Mon	Tue	Wed	Thur	Fri	Sat	Sun	Total	Achievement Bar
	Date									
	Goal									25 50 75 100
	Actual									
	Goal									25 50 75 100
	Actual									
	Goal									25 50 75 100
	Actual									
	Goal									25 50 75 100
	Actual									
	Goal									25 50 75 100
	Actual									

5-Minute Mindset

Step 6: Provide Ongoing Motivation
Step 7: Interpret Results and Adjust Accordingly
Step 8: Celebrate Your Success
Step 9: Arrive at Your Destination

Date	Entries

5-Minute Mindset

Step 6: Provide Ongoing Motivation
Step 7: Interpret Results and Adjust Accordingly
Step 8: Celebrate Your Success
Step 9: Arrive at Your Destination

Date	Entries

The 5-Minute Mindset

Step 6: Provide Ongoing Motivation
Step 7: Interpret Results and Adjust Accordingly
Step 8: Celebrate Your Success
Step 9: Arrive at Your Destination

Date	Entries

The 5-Minute Mindset

Step 6: Provide Ongoing Motivation
Step 7: Interpret Results and Adjust Accordingly
Step 8: Celebrate Your Success
Step 9: Arrive at Your Destination

Date	Entries

The 5-Minute Mindset

Forms for # 6

(After you decide what area you want to work on, come back to this page and fill it in.)

_____

_____

_____

	Step 1: Make A Decision
The 5-Minute Mindset	**Step 1: Make A Decision**

What area do you want to work on?
(Example: Spiritual, Physical, Social, Emotional, Educational, Financial)

5-Minute Mindset (The)

Step 2: Write Your Story and Find Your 'Whys'

What area in your life did you decide to work on?

Make a list of your reasons for this decision or write stories that illustrate why this decision is important to you.

5-Minute Mindset

The

Step 2: Write Your Story and Find Your 'Whys'

What area in your life did you decide to work on?

Make a list of your reasons for this decision or write stories that illustrate why this decision is important to you.

The 5-Minute Mindset

Step 3: Set Goals
Long Term and Intermediate

Long Term Goal:	Deadline	Goal	Actual

Achievement Bar			
25%	50%	75%	100%

Intermediate Goals or Tasks	Deadline	Goal	Actual	Achievement Bar
				25 50 75 100
				25 50 75 100
				25 50 75 100
				25 50 75 100
				25 50 75 100
				25 50 75 100
				25 50 75 100
				25 50 75 100
				25 50 75 100
				25 50 75 100
				25 50 75 100
				25 50 75 100
				25 50 75 100
				25 50 75 100
				25 50 75 100
				25 50 75 100
				25 50 75 100
				25 50 75 100

Step 4: Design a Plan

The 5-Minute Mindset

Brainstorm; Resources,
Principles, Rules and Guidelines

Goal / Due Date:

What resources of information are available to you? Do you know any experts? What are
the hard and fast rules that will lead to success? What are the core principles? What
guidelines are you going to set? How are you going to achieve your goal?

Priority	Entries

The 5-Minute Mindset

Step 4: Design a Plan
Step 5: Implement a Plan
Daily/Weekly Goal Tracker

Month_____

GOAL(S)

Daily/Weekly Tasks		Mon	Tue	Wed	Thur	Fri	Sat	Sun	Total	Achievement Bar
	Date									
	Goal									25 50 75 100
	Actual									
	Goal									25 50 75 100
	Actual									
	Goal									25 50 75 100
	Actual									
	Goal									25 50 75 100
	Actual									
	Goal									25 50 75 100
	Actual									

Daily/Weekly Tasks		Mon	Tue	Wed	Thur	Fri	Sat	Sun	Total	Achievement Bar
	Date									
	Goal									25 50 75 100
	Actual									
	Goal									25 50 75 100
	Actual									
	Goal									25 50 75 100
	Actual									
	Goal									25 50 75 100
	Actual									
	Goal									25 50 75 100
	Actual									

Daily/Weekly Tasks		Mon	Tue	Wed	Thur	Fri	Sat	Sun	Total	Achievement Bar
	Date									
	Goal									25 50 75 100
	Actual									
	Goal									25 50 75 100
	Actual									
	Goal									25 50 75 100
	Actual									
	Goal									25 50 75 100
	Actual									
	Goal									25 50 75 100
	Actual									

5-Minute Mindset

Step 4: Design a Plan
Step 5: Implement a Plan   **Month_____**
Daily/Weekly Goal Tracker

GOAL(S)

Daily/Weekly Tasks		Mon	Tue	Wed	Thur	Fri	Sat	Sun	Total	Achievement Bar
	Date									
	Goal									25 50 75 100
	Actual									
	Goal									25 50 75 100
	Actual									
	Goal									25 50 75 100
	Actual									
	Goal									25 50 75 100
	Actual									
	Goal									25 50 75 100
	Actual									

Daily/Weekly Tasks		Mon	Tue	Wed	Thur	Fri	Sat	Sun	Total	Achievement Bar
	Date									
	Goal									25 50 75 100
	Actual									
	Goal									25 50 75 100
	Actual									
	Goal									25 50 75 100
	Actual									
	Goal									25 50 75 100
	Actual									
	Goal									25 50 75 100
	Actual									

Daily/Weekly Tasks		Mon	Tue	Wed	Thur	Fri	Sat	Sun	Total	Achievement Bar
	Date									
	Goal									25 50 75 100
	Actual									
	Goal									25 50 75 100
	Actual									
	Goal									25 50 75 100
	Actual									
	Goal									25 50 75 100
	Actual									
	Goal									25 50 75 100
	Actual									

The 5-Minute Mindset

Step 4: Design a Plan
Step 5: Implement a Plan

Daily/Weekly Goal Tracker

Month_____

GOAL(S)

Daily/Weekly Tasks	Date	Mon	Tue	Wed	Thur	Fri	Sat	Sun	Total	Achievement Bar
	Goal									25 50 75 100
	Actual									
	Goal									25 50 75 100
	Actual									
	Goal									25 50 75 100
	Actual									
	Goal									25 50 75 100
	Actual									
	Goal									25 50 75 100
	Actual									

Daily/Weekly Tasks	Date	Mon	Tue	Wed	Thur	Fri	Sat	Sun	Total	Achievement Bar
	Goal									25 50 75 100
	Actual									
	Goal									25 50 75 100
	Actual									
	Goal									25 50 75 100
	Actual									
	Goal									25 50 75 100
	Actual									
	Goal									25 50 75 100
	Actual									

Daily/Weekly Tasks	Date	Mon	Tue	Wed	Thur	Fri	Sat	Sun	Total	Achievement Bar
	Goal									25 50 75 100
	Actual									
	Goal									25 50 75 100
	Actual									
	Goal									25 50 75 100
	Actual									
	Goal									25 50 75 100
	Actual									

The 5-Minute Mindset

Step 4: Design a Plan
Step 5: Implement a Plan
Daily/Weekly Goal Tracker

Month_____

GOAL(S)

Daily/Weekly Tasks		Mon	Tue	Wed	Thur	Fri	Sat	Sun	Total	Achievement Bar
	Date									
	Goal									25 50 75 100
	Actual									
	Goal									25 50 75 100
	Actual									
	Goal									25 50 75 100
	Actual									
	Goal									25 50 75 100
	Actual									
	Goal									25 50 75 100
	Actual									

Daily/Weekly Tasks		Mon	Tue	Wed	Thur	Fri	Sat	Sun	Total	Achievement Bar
	Date									
	Goal									25 50 75 100
	Actual									
	Goal									25 50 75 100
	Actual									
	Goal									25 50 75 100
	Actual									
	Goal									25 50 75 100
	Actual									
	Goal									25 50 75 100
	Actual									

Daily/Weekly Tasks		Mon	Tue	Wed	Thur	Fri	Sat	Sun	Total	Achievement Bar
	Date									
	Goal									25 50 75 100
	Actual									
	Goal									25 50 75 100
	Actual									
	Goal									25 50 75 100
	Actual									
	Goal									25 50 75 100
	Actual									
	Goal									25 50 75 100
	Actual									

5-Minute Mindset (The)

Step 4: Design a Plan
Step 5: Implement a Plan

Month_____

Daily/Weekly Goal Tracker

GOAL(S)

Daily/Weekly Tasks		Mon	Tue	Wed	Thur	Fri	Sat	Sun	Total	Achievement Bar
	Date									
	Goal									25 50 75 100
	Actual									
	Goal									25 50 75 100
	Actual									
	Goal									25 50 75 100
	Actual									
	Goal									25 50 75 100
	Actual									
	Goal									25 50 75 100
	Actual									

Daily/Weekly Tasks		Mon	Tue	Wed	Thur	Fri	Sat	Sun	Total	Achievement Bar
	Date									
	Goal									25 50 75 100
	Actual									
	Goal									25 50 75 100
	Actual									
	Goal									25 50 75 100
	Actual									
	Goal									25 50 75 100
	Actual									
	Goal									25 50 75 100
	Actual									

Daily/Weekly Tasks		Mon	Tue	Wed	Thur	Fri	Sat	Sun	Total	Achievement Bar
	Date									
	Goal									25 50 75 100
	Actual									
	Goal									25 50 75 100
	Actual									
	Goal									25 50 75 100
	Actual									
	Goal									25 50 75 100
	Actual									
	Goal									25 50 75 100
	Actual									

Step 4: Design a Plan
Step 5: Implement a Plan

5-Minute Mindset The

Daily/Weekly Goal Tracker

Month_____

GOAL(S)

Daily/Weekly Tasks		Mon	Tue	Wed	Thur	Fri	Sat	Sun	Total	Achievement Bar
	Date									
	Goal									25 50 75 100
	Actual									
	Goal									25 50 75 100
	Actual									
	Goal									25 50 75 100
	Actual									
	Goal									25 50 75 100
	Actual									
	Goal									25 50 75 100
	Actual									

Daily/Weekly Tasks		Mon	Tue	Wed	Thur	Fri	Sat	Sun	Total	Achievement Bar
	Date									
	Goal									25 50 75 100
	Actual									
	Goal									25 50 75 100
	Actual									
	Goal									25 50 75 100
	Actual									
	Goal									25 50 75 100
	Actual									
	Goal									25 50 75 100
	Actual									

Daily/Weekly Tasks		Mon	Tue	Wed	Thur	Fri	Sat	Sun	Total	Achievement Bar
	Date									
	Goal									25 50 75 100
	Actual									
	Goal									25 50 75 100
	Actual									
	Goal									25 50 75 100
	Actual									
	Goal									25 50 75 100
	Actual									
	Goal									25 50 75 100
	Actual									

The 5-Minute Mindset

Step 4: Design a Plan
Step 5: Implement a Plan
Daily/Weekly Goal Tracker

Month_____

GOAL(S)

Daily/Weekly Tasks		Mon	Tue	Wed	Thur	Fri	Sat	Sun	Total	Achievement Bar
	Date									
	Goal									25 50 75 100
	Actual									
	Goal									25 50 75 100
	Actual									
	Goal									25 50 75 100
	Actual									
	Goal									25 50 75 100
	Actual									
	Goal									25 50 75 100
	Actual									

Daily/Weekly Tasks		Mon	Tue	Wed	Thur	Fri	Sat	Sun	Total	Achievement Bar
	Date									
	Goal									25 50 75 100
	Actual									
	Goal									25 50 75 100
	Actual									
	Goal									25 50 75 100
	Actual									
	Goal									25 50 75 100
	Actual									
	Goal									25 50 75 100
	Actual									

Daily/Weekly Tasks		Mon	Tue	Wed	Thur	Fri	Sat	Sun	Total	Achievement Bar
	Date									
	Goal									25 50 75 100
	Actual									
	Goal									25 50 75 100
	Actual									
	Goal									25 50 75 100
	Actual									
	Goal									25 50 75 100
	Actual									

5-Minute Mindset (The)

Step 4: Design a Plan
Step 5: Implement a Plan   Month_____
Daily/Weekly Goal Tracker

GOAL(S)

Daily/Weekly Tasks		Mon	Tue	Wed	Thur	Fri	Sat	Sun	Total	Achievement Bar
	Date									
	Goal									25 50 75 100
	Actual									
	Goal									25 50 75 100
	Actual									
	Goal									25 50 75 100
	Actual									
	Goal									25 50 75 100
	Actual									
	Goal									25 50 75 100
	Actual									

Daily/Weekly Tasks		Mon	Tue	Wed	Thur	Fri	Sat	Sun	Total	Achievement Bar
	Date									
	Goal									25 50 75 100
	Actual									
	Goal									25 50 75 100
	Actual									
	Goal									25 50 75 100
	Actual									
	Goal									25 50 75 100
	Actual									
	Goal									25 50 75 100
	Actual									

Daily/Weekly Tasks		Mon	Tue	Wed	Thur	Fri	Sat	Sun	Total	Achievement Bar
	Date									
	Goal									25 50 75 100
	Actual									
	Goal									25 50 75 100
	Actual									
	Goal									25 50 75 100
	Actual									
	Goal									25 50 75 100
	Actual									
	Goal									25 50 75 100
	Actual									

The 5-Minute Mindset

Step 4: Design a Plan
Step 5: Implement a Plan
Daily/Weekly Goal Tracker

Month_____

GOAL(S)

Daily/Weekly Tasks		Mon	Tue	Wed	Thur	Fri	Sat	Sun	Total	Achievement Bar
	Date									
	Goal									25 50 75 100
	Actual									
	Goal									25 50 75 100
	Actual									
	Goal									25 50 75 100
	Actual									
	Goal									25 50 75 100
	Actual									
	Goal									25 50 75 100
	Actual									

Daily/Weekly Tasks		Mon	Tue	Wed	Thur	Fri	Sat	Sun	Total	Achievement Bar
	Date									
	Goal									25 50 75 100
	Actual									
	Goal									25 50 75 100
	Actual									
	Goal									25 50 75 100
	Actual									
	Goal									25 50 75 100
	Actual									
	Goal									25 50 75 100
	Actual									

Daily/Weekly Tasks		Mon	Tue	Wed	Thur	Fri	Sat	Sun	Total	Achievement Bar
	Date									
	Goal									25 50 75 100
	Actual									
	Goal									25 50 75 100
	Actual									
	Goal									25 50 75 100
	Actual									
	Goal									25 50 75 100
	Actual									
	Goal									25 50 75 100
	Actual									

| The 5-Minute Mindset | **Step 4: Design a Plan** **Step 5: Implement a Plan** Daily/Weekly Goal Tracker | Month_____ |

GOAL(S)

Daily/Weekly Tasks		Mon	Tue	Wed	Thur	Fri	Sat	Sun	Total	Achievement Bar
	Date									
	Goal									25 50 75 100
	Actual									
	Goal									25 50 75 100
	Actual									
	Goal									25 50 75 100
	Actual									
	Goal									25 50 75 100
	Actual									
	Goal									25 50 75 100
	Actual									

Daily/Weekly Tasks		Mon	Tue	Wed	Thur	Fri	Sat	Sun	Total	Achievement Bar
	Date									
	Goal									25 50 75 100
	Actual									
	Goal									25 50 75 100
	Actual									
	Goal									25 50 75 100
	Actual									
	Goal									25 50 75 100
	Actual									
	Goal									25 50 75 100
	Actual									

Daily/Weekly Tasks		Mon	Tue	Wed	Thur	Fri	Sat	Sun	Total	Achievement Bar
	Date									
	Goal									25 50 75 100
	Actual									
	Goal									25 50 75 100
	Actual									
	Goal									25 50 75 100
	Actual									
	Goal									25 50 75 100
	Actual									
	Goal									25 50 75 100
	Actual									

The 5-Minute Mindset

Step 4: Design a Plan
Step 5: Implement a Plan　　Month_____
Daily/Weekly Goal Tracker

GOAL(S)

Daily/Weekly Tasks		Mon	Tue	Wed	Thur	Fri	Sat	Sun	Total	Achievement Bar
	Date									
	Goal									25 50 75 100
	Actual									
	Goal									25 50 75 100
	Actual									
	Goal									25 50 75 100
	Actual									
	Goal									25 50 75 100
	Actual									
	Goal									25 50 75 100
	Actual									

Daily/Weekly Tasks		Mon	Tue	Wed	Thur	Fri	Sat	Sun	Total	Achievement Bar
	Date									
	Goal									25 50 75 100
	Actual									
	Goal									25 50 75 100
	Actual									
	Goal									25 50 75 100
	Actual									
	Goal									25 50 75 100
	Actual									
	Goal									25 50 75 100
	Actual									

Daily/Weekly Tasks		Mon	Tue	Wed	Thur	Fri	Sat	Sun	Total	Achievement Bar
	Date									
	Goal									25 50 75 100
	Actual									
	Goal									25 50 75 100
	Actual									
	Goal									25 50 75 100
	Actual									
	Goal									25 50 75 100
	Actual									

5-Minute Mindset (The)

Step 4: Design a Plan
Step 5: Implement a Plan
Daily/Weekly Goal Tracker

Month_____

GOAL(S)

Daily/Weekly Tasks		Mon	Tue	Wed	Thur	Fri	Sat	Sun	Total	Achievement Bar
	Date									
	Goal									25 50 75 100
	Actual									
	Goal									25 50 75 100
	Actual									
	Goal									25 50 75 100
	Actual									
	Goal									25 50 75 100
	Actual									
	Goal									25 50 75 100
	Actual									

Daily/Weekly Tasks		Mon	Tue	Wed	Thur	Fri	Sat	Sun	Total	Achievement Bar
	Date									
	Goal									25 50 75 100
	Actual									
	Goal									25 50 75 100
	Actual									
	Goal									25 50 75 100
	Actual									
	Goal									25 50 75 100
	Actual									
	Goal									25 50 75 100
	Actual									

Daily/Weekly Tasks		Mon	Tue	Wed	Thur	Fri	Sat	Sun	Total	Achievement Bar
	Date									
	Goal									25 50 75 100
	Actual									
	Goal									25 50 75 100
	Actual									
	Goal									25 50 75 100
	Actual									
	Goal									25 50 75 100
	Actual									
	Goal									25 50 75 100
	Actual									

5-Minute Mindset
The

Step 4: Design a Plan
Step 5: Implement a Plan   Month_____
Daily/Weekly Goal Tracker

GOAL(S)

Daily/Weekly Tasks		Mon	Tue	Wed	Thur	Fri	Sat	Sun	Total	Achievement Bar
	Date									
	Goal									25 50 75 100
	Actual									
	Goal									25 50 75 100
	Actual									
	Goal									25 50 75 100
	Actual									
	Goal									25 50 75 100
	Actual									
	Goal									25 50 75 100
	Actual									

Daily/Weekly Tasks		Mon	Tue	Wed	Thur	Fri	Sat	Sun	Total	Achievement Bar
	Date									
	Goal									25 50 75 100
	Actual									
	Goal									25 50 75 100
	Actual									
	Goal									25 50 75 100
	Actual									
	Goal									25 50 75 100
	Actual									
	Goal									25 50 75 100
	Actual									

Daily/Weekly Tasks		Mon	Tue	Wed	Thur	Fri	Sat	Sun	Total	Achievement Bar
	Date									
	Goal									25 50 75 100
	Actual									
	Goal									25 50 75 100
	Actual									
	Goal									25 50 75 100
	Actual									
	Goal									25 50 75 100
	Actual									
	Goal									25 50 75 100
	Actual									

The 5-Minute Mindset

Step 4: Design a Plan
Step 5: Implement a Plan

Month_____

Daily/Weekly Goal Tracker

GOAL(S)

Daily/Weekly Tasks		Mon	Tue	Wed	Thur	Fri	Sat	Sun	Total	Achievement Bar
	Date									
	Goal									25 50 75 100
	Actual									
	Goal									25 50 75 100
	Actual									
	Goal									25 50 75 100
	Actual									
	Goal									25 50 75 100
	Actual									
	Goal									25 50 75 100
	Actual									
Daily/Weekly Tasks		**Mon**	**Tue**	**Wed**	**Thur**	**Fri**	**Sat**	**Sun**	**Total**	Achievement Bar
	Date									
	Goal									25 50 75 100
	Actual									
	Goal									25 50 75 100
	Actual									
	Goal									25 50 75 100
	Actual									
	Goal									25 50 75 100
	Actual									
	Goal									25 50 75 100
	Actual									
Daily/Weekly Tasks		**Mon**	**Tue**	**Wed**	**Thur**	**Fri**	**Sat**	**Sun**	**Total**	Achievement Bar
	Date									
	Goal									25 50 75 100
	Actual									
	Goal									25 50 75 100
	Actual									
	Goal									25 50 75 100
	Actual									
	Goal									25 50 75 100
	Actual									
	Goal									25 50 75 100
	Actual									

The 5-Minute Mindset

Step 4: Design a Plan
Step 5: Implement a Plan
Daily/Weekly Goal Tracker

Month_____

GOAL(S)

Daily/Weekly Tasks		Mon	Tue	Wed	Thur	Fri	Sat	Sun	Total	Achievement Bar
	Date									
	Goal									25 50 75 100
	Actual									
	Goal									25 50 75 100
	Actual									
	Goal									25 50 75 100
	Actual									
	Goal									25 50 75 100
	Actual									
	Goal									25 50 75 100
	Actual									

Daily/Weekly Tasks		Mon	Tue	Wed	Thur	Fri	Sat	Sun	Total	Achievement Bar
	Date									
	Goal									25 50 75 100
	Actual									
	Goal									25 50 75 100
	Actual									
	Goal									25 50 75 100
	Actual									
	Goal									25 50 75 100
	Actual									
	Goal									25 50 75 100
	Actual									

Daily/Weekly Tasks		Mon	Tue	Wed	Thur	Fri	Sat	Sun	Total	Achievement Bar
	Date									
	Goal									25 50 75 100
	Actual									
	Goal									25 50 75 100
	Actual									
	Goal									25 50 75 100
	Actual									
	Goal									25 50 75 100
	Actual									
	Goal									25 50 75 100
	Actual									

5-Minute Mindset (The)

Step 4: Design a Plan
Step 5: Implement a Plan
Daily/Weekly Goal Tracker

Month_____

GOAL(S)

Daily/Weekly Tasks		Mon	Tue	Wed	Thur	Fri	Sat	Sun	Total	Achievement Bar
	Date									
	Goal									25 50 75 100
	Actual									
	Goal									25 50 75 100
	Actual									
	Goal									25 50 75 100
	Actual									
	Goal									25 50 75 100
	Actual									
	Goal									25 50 75 100
	Actual									

Daily/Weekly Tasks		Mon	Tue	Wed	Thur	Fri	Sat	Sun	Total	Achievement Bar
	Date									
	Goal									25 50 75 100
	Actual									
	Goal									25 50 75 100
	Actual									
	Goal									25 50 75 100
	Actual									
	Goal									25 50 75 100
	Actual									
	Goal									25 50 75 100
	Actual									

Daily/Weekly Tasks		Mon	Tue	Wed	Thur	Fri	Sat	Sun	Total	Achievement Bar
	Date									
	Goal									25 50 75 100
	Actual									
	Goal									25 50 75 100
	Actual									
	Goal									25 50 75 100
	Actual									
	Goal									25 50 75 100
	Actual									
	Goal									25 50 75 100
	Actual									

The 5-Minute Mindset

Step 4: Design a Plan
Step 5: Implement a Plan
Daily/Weekly Goal Tracker

Month_____

GOAL(S)

Daily/Weekly Tasks	Date	Mon	Tue	Wed	Thur	Fri	Sat	Sun	Total	Achievement Bar
	Goal									25 50 75 100
	Actual									
	Goal									25 50 75 100
	Actual									
	Goal									25 50 75 100
	Actual									
	Goal									25 50 75 100
	Actual									
	Goal									25 50 75 100
	Actual									

Daily/Weekly Tasks	Date	Mon	Tue	Wed	Thur	Fri	Sat	Sun	Total	Achievement Bar
	Goal									25 50 75 100
	Actual									
	Goal									25 50 75 100
	Actual									
	Goal									25 50 75 100
	Actual									
	Goal									25 50 75 100
	Actual									
	Goal									25 50 75 100
	Actual									

Daily/Weekly Tasks	Date	Mon	Tue	Wed	Thur	Fri	Sat	Sun	Total	Achievement Bar
	Goal									25 50 75 100
	Actual									
	Goal									25 50 75 100
	Actual									
	Goal									25 50 75 100
	Actual									
	Goal									25 50 75 100
	Actual									

Step 4: Design a Plan
Step 5: Implement a Plan

The 5-Minute Mindset

Month_____

Daily/Weekly Goal Tracker

GOAL(S)

Daily/Weekly Tasks		Mon	Tue	Wed	Thur	Fri	Sat	Sun	Total	Achievement Bar
	Date									
	Goal									25 50 75 100
	Actual									
	Goal									25 50 75 100
	Actual									
	Goal									25 50 75 100
	Actual									
	Goal									25 50 75 100
	Actual									
	Goal									25 50 75 100
	Actual									

Daily/Weekly Tasks		Mon	Tue	Wed	Thur	Fri	Sat	Sun	Total	Achievement Bar
	Date									
	Goal									25 50 75 100
	Actual									
	Goal									25 50 75 100
	Actual									
	Goal									25 50 75 100
	Actual									
	Goal									25 50 75 100
	Actual									
	Goal									25 50 75 100
	Actual									

Daily/Weekly Tasks		Mon	Tue	Wed	Thur	Fri	Sat	Sun	Total	Achievement Bar
	Date									
	Goal									25 50 75 100
	Actual									
	Goal									25 50 75 100
	Actual									
	Goal									25 50 75 100
	Actual									
	Goal									25 50 75 100
	Actual									
	Goal									25 50 75 100
	Actual									

The 5-Minute Mindset

Step 6: Provide Ongoing Motivation
Step 7: Interpret Results and Adjust Accordingly
Step 8: Celebrate Your Success
Step 9: Arrive at Your Destination

Date	Entries

The 5-Minute Mindset

Step 6: Provide Ongoing Motivation
Step 7: Interpret Results and Adjust Accordingly
Step 8: Celebrate Your Success
Step 9: Arrive at Your Destination

Date	Entries

The 5-Minute Mindset

Step 6: Provide Ongoing Motivation
Step 7: Interpret Results and Adjust Accordingly
Step 8: Celebrate Your Success
Step 9: Arrive at Your Destination

Date	Entries

The 5-Minute Mindset

Step 6: Provide Ongoing Motivation
Step 7: Interpret Results and Adjust Accordingly
Step 8: Celebrate Your Success
Step 9: Arrive at Your Destination

Date	Entries

The 5-Minute Mindset

Forms for # 7

(After you decide what area you want to work on, come back to this page and fill it in.)

_____

_____

_____

The 5-Minute Mindset   Step 1: Make A Decision

What area do you want to work on?
(Example: Spiritual, Physical, Social, Emotional, Educational, Financial)

The 5-Minute Mindset

Step 2: Write Your Story and Find Your 'Whys'

What area in your life did you decide to work on?

Make a list of your reasons for this decision or write stories that illustrate why this decision is important to you.

5-Minute Mindset
The

**Step 2: Write Your Story
and Find Your 'Whys'**

What area in your life did you decide to work on?

**Make a list of your reasons for this decision or write stories
that illustrate why this decision is important to you.**

The 5-Minute Mindset

Step 3: Set Goals
Long Term and Intermediate

Long Term Goal:	Deadline	Goal	Actual

Achievement Bar				
	25%	50%	75%	100%

Intermediate Goals or Tasks	Deadline	Goal	Actual	Achievement Bar
				25 50 75 100
				25 50 75 100
				25 50 75 100
				25 50 75 100
				25 50 75 100
				25 50 75 100
				25 50 75 100
				25 50 75 100
				25 50 75 100
				25 50 75 100
				25 50 75 100
				25 50 75 100
				25 50 75 100
				25 50 75 100
				25 50 75 100
				25 50 75 100
				25 50 75 100

The 5-Minute Mindset

Step 4: Design a Plan
Brainstorm; Resources,
Principles, Rules and Guidelines

Goal / Due Date:

What resources of information are available to you? Do you know any experts? What are the hard and fast rules that will lead to success? What are the core principles? What guidelines are you going to set? How are you going to achieve your goal?

Priority	Entries

5 The Minute Mindset

Step 4: Design a Plan
Step 5: Implement a Plan   Month_____
Daily/Weekly Goal Tracker

GOAL(S)

Daily/Weekly Tasks		Mon	Tue	Wed	Thur	Fri	Sat	Sun	Total	Achievement Bar
	Date									
	Goal									25 50 75 100
	Actual									
	Goal									25 50 75 100
	Actual									
	Goal									25 50 75 100
	Actual									
	Goal									25 50 75 100
	Actual									
	Goal									25 50 75 100
	Actual									

Daily/Weekly Tasks		Mon	Tue	Wed	Thur	Fri	Sat	Sun	Total	Achievement Bar
	Date									
	Goal									25 50 75 100
	Actual									
	Goal									25 50 75 100
	Actual									
	Goal									25 50 75 100
	Actual									
	Goal									25 50 75 100
	Actual									
	Goal									25 50 75 100
	Actual									

Daily/Weekly Tasks		Mon	Tue	Wed	Thur	Fri	Sat	Sun	Total	Achievement Bar
	Date									
	Goal									25 50 75 100
	Actual									
	Goal									25 50 75 100
	Actual									
	Goal									25 50 75 100
	Actual									
	Goal									25 50 75 100
	Actual									
	Goal									25 50 75 100
	Actual									

The 5-Minute Mindset

Step 4: Design a Plan
Step 5: Implement a Plan
Daily/Weekly Goal Tracker

Month_____

GOAL(S)

Daily/Weekly Tasks		Mon	Tue	Wed	Thur	Fri	Sat	Sun	Total	Achievement Bar
	Date									
	Goal									25 50 75 100
	Actual									
	Goal									25 50 75 100
	Actual									
	Goal									25 50 75 100
	Actual									
	Goal									25 50 75 100
	Actual									
	Goal									25 50 75 100
	Actual									

Daily/Weekly Tasks		Mon	Tue	Wed	Thur	Fri	Sat	Sun	Total	Achievement Bar
	Date									
	Goal									25 50 75 100
	Actual									
	Goal									25 50 75 100
	Actual									
	Goal									25 50 75 100
	Actual									
	Goal									25 50 75 100
	Actual									
	Goal									25 50 75 100
	Actual									

Daily/Weekly Tasks		Mon	Tue	Wed	Thur	Fri	Sat	Sun	Total	Achievement Bar
	Date									
	Goal									25 50 75 100
	Actual									
	Goal									25 50 75 100
	Actual									
	Goal									25 50 75 100
	Actual									
	Goal									25 50 75 100
	Actual									
	Goal									25 50 75 100
	Actual									

5-Minute Mindset
The

Step 4: Design a Plan
Step 5: Implement a Plan   Month_____
Daily/Weekly Goal Tracker

GOAL(S)

Daily/Weekly Tasks		Mon	Tue	Wed	Thur	Fri	Sat	Sun	Total	Achievement Bar
	Date									
	Goal									25 50 75 100
	Actual									
	Goal									25 50 75 100
	Actual									
	Goal									25 50 75 100
	Actual									
	Goal									25 50 75 100
	Actual									
	Goal									25 50 75 100
	Actual									

Daily/Weekly Tasks		Mon	Tue	Wed	Thur	Fri	Sat	Sun	Total	Achievement Bar
	Date									
	Goal									25 50 75 100
	Actual									
	Goal									25 50 75 100
	Actual									
	Goal									25 50 75 100
	Actual									
	Goal									25 50 75 100
	Actual									
	Goal									25 50 75 100
	Actual									

Daily/Weekly Tasks		Mon	Tue	Wed	Thur	Fri	Sat	Sun	Total	Achievement Bar
	Date									
	Goal									25 50 75 100
	Actual									
	Goal									25 50 75 100
	Actual									
	Goal									25 50 75 100
	Actual									
	Goal									25 50 75 100
	Actual									
	Goal									25 50 75 100
	Actual									

The 5-Minute Mindset

Step 4: Design a Plan
Step 5: Implement a Plan

Month_____

Daily/Weekly Goal Tracker

GOAL(S)

Daily/Weekly Tasks		Mon	Tue	Wed	Thur	Fri	Sat	Sun	Total	Achievement Bar
	Date									
	Goal									25 50 75 100
	Actual									
	Goal									25 50 75 100
	Actual									
	Goal									25 50 75 100
	Actual									
	Goal									25 50 75 100
	Actual									
	Goal									25 50 75 100
	Actual									

Daily/Weekly Tasks		Mon	Tue	Wed	Thur	Fri	Sat	Sun	Total	Achievement Bar
	Date									
	Goal									25 50 75 100
	Actual									
	Goal									25 50 75 100
	Actual									
	Goal									25 50 75 100
	Actual									
	Goal									25 50 75 100
	Actual									
	Goal									25 50 75 100
	Actual									

Daily/Weekly Tasks		Mon	Tue	Wed	Thur	Fri	Sat	Sun	Total	Achievement Bar
	Date									
	Goal									25 50 75 100
	Actual									
	Goal									25 50 75 100
	Actual									
	Goal									25 50 75 100
	Actual									
	Goal									25 50 75 100
	Actual									
	Goal									25 50 75 100
	Actual									

5-Minute Mindset

Step 4: Design a Plan
Step 5: Implement a Plan
Daily/Weekly Goal Tracker

Month_____

GOAL(S)

Daily/Weekly Tasks	Date	Mon	Tue	Wed	Thur	Fri	Sat	Sun	Total	Achievement Bar
	Goal									25 50 75 100
	Actual									
	Goal									25 50 75 100
	Actual									
	Goal									25 50 75 100
	Actual									
	Goal									25 50 75 100
	Actual									
	Goal									25 50 75 100
	Actual									

Daily/Weekly Tasks	Date	Mon	Tue	Wed	Thur	Fri	Sat	Sun	Total	Achievement Bar
	Goal									25 50 75 100
	Actual									
	Goal									25 50 75 100
	Actual									
	Goal									25 50 75 100
	Actual									
	Goal									25 50 75 100
	Actual									
	Goal									25 50 75 100
	Actual									

Daily/Weekly Tasks	Date	Mon	Tue	Wed	Thur	Fri	Sat	Sun	Total	Achievement Bar
	Goal									25 50 75 100
	Actual									
	Goal									25 50 75 100
	Actual									
	Goal									25 50 75 100
	Actual									
	Goal									25 50 75 100
	Actual									
	Goal									25 50 75 100
	Actual									

Step 4: Design a Plan
Step 5: Implement a Plan
Daily/Weekly Goal Tracker

5-Minute Mindset

Month_____

GOAL(S)

Daily/Weekly Tasks		Mon	Tue	Wed	Thur	Fri	Sat	Sun	Total	Achievement Bar
	Date									
	Goal									25 50 75 100
	Actual									
	Goal									25 50 75 100
	Actual									
	Goal									25 50 75 100
	Actual									
	Goal									25 50 75 100
	Actual									
	Goal									25 50 75 100
	Actual									

Daily/Weekly Tasks		Mon	Tue	Wed	Thur	Fri	Sat	Sun	Total	Achievement Bar
	Date									
	Goal									25 50 75 100
	Actual									
	Goal									25 50 75 100
	Actual									
	Goal									25 50 75 100
	Actual									
	Goal									25 50 75 100
	Actual									
	Goal									25 50 75 100
	Actual									

Daily/Weekly Tasks		Mon	Tue	Wed	Thur	Fri	Sat	Sun	Total	Achievement Bar
	Date									
	Goal									25 50 75 100
	Actual									
	Goal									25 50 75 100
	Actual									
	Goal									25 50 75 100
	Actual									
	Goal									25 50 75 100
	Actual									
	Goal									25 50 75 100
	Actual									

The 5-Minute Mindset

Step 4: Design a Plan
Step 5: Implement a Plan
Daily/Weekly Goal Tracker

Month_____

GOAL(S)

Daily/Weekly Tasks	Date	Mon	Tue	Wed	Thur	Fri	Sat	Sun	Total	Achievement Bar
	Goal									25 50 75 100
	Actual									
	Goal									25 50 75 100
	Actual									
	Goal									25 50 75 100
	Actual									
	Goal									25 50 75 100
	Actual									
	Goal									25 50 75 100
	Actual									

Daily/Weekly Tasks	Date	Mon	Tue	Wed	Thur	Fri	Sat	Sun	Total	Achievement Bar
	Goal									25 50 75 100
	Actual									
	Goal									25 50 75 100
	Actual									
	Goal									25 50 75 100
	Actual									
	Goal									25 50 75 100
	Actual									
	Goal									25 50 75 100
	Actual									

Daily/Weekly Tasks	Date	Mon	Tue	Wed	Thur	Fri	Sat	Sun	Total	Achievement Bar
	Goal									25 50 75 100
	Actual									
	Goal									25 50 75 100
	Actual									
	Goal									25 50 75 100
	Actual									
	Goal									25 50 75 100
	Actual									
	Goal									25 50 75 100
	Actual									

5-Minute Mindset

Step 4: Design a Plan
Step 5: Implement a Plan   Month_____
Daily/Weekly Goal Tracker

GOAL(S)

Daily/Weekly Tasks		Mon	Tue	Wed	Thur	Fri	Sat	Sun	Total	Achievement Bar
	Date									
	Goal									25 50 75 100
	Actual									
	Goal									25 50 75 100
	Actual									
	Goal									25 50 75 100
	Actual									
	Goal									25 50 75 100
	Actual									
	Goal									25 50 75 100
	Actual									

Daily/Weekly Tasks		Mon	Tue	Wed	Thur	Fri	Sat	Sun	Total	Achievement Bar
	Date									
	Goal									25 50 75 100
	Actual									
	Goal									25 50 75 100
	Actual									
	Goal									25 50 75 100
	Actual									
	Goal									25 50 75 100
	Actual									
	Goal									25 50 75 100
	Actual									

Daily/Weekly Tasks		Mon	Tue	Wed	Thur	Fri	Sat	Sun	Total	Achievement Bar
	Date									
	Goal									25 50 75 100
	Actual									
	Goal									25 50 75 100
	Actual									
	Goal									25 50 75 100
	Actual									
	Goal									25 50 75 100
	Actual									
	Goal									25 50 75 100
	Actual									

5 The -Minute Mindset

Step 4: Design a Plan
Step 5: Implement a Plan
Daily/Weekly Goal Tracker

Month_____

GOAL(S)

Daily/Weekly Tasks	Date	Mon	Tue	Wed	Thur	Fri	Sat	Sun	Total	Achievement Bar
	Goal									25 50 75 100
	Actual									
	Goal									25 50 75 100
	Actual									
	Goal									25 50 75 100
	Actual									
	Goal									25 50 75 100
	Actual									
	Goal									25 50 75 100
	Actual									

Daily/Weekly Tasks	Date	Mon	Tue	Wed	Thur	Fri	Sat	Sun	Total	Achievement Bar
	Goal									25 50 75 100
	Actual									
	Goal									25 50 75 100
	Actual									
	Goal									25 50 75 100
	Actual									
	Goal									25 50 75 100
	Actual									
	Goal									25 50 75 100
	Actual									

Daily/Weekly Tasks	Date	Mon	Tue	Wed	Thur	Fri	Sat	Sun	Total	Achievement Bar
	Goal									25 50 75 100
	Actual									
	Goal									25 50 75 100
	Actual									
	Goal									25 50 75 100
	Actual									
	Goal									25 50 75 100
	Actual									
	Goal									25 50 75 100
	Actual									

5-Minute Mindset
Step 4: Design a Plan
Step 5: Implement a Plan
Daily/Weekly Goal Tracker

Month_____

GOAL(S)

Daily/Weekly Tasks		Mon	Tue	Wed	Thur	Fri	Sat	Sun	Total	Achievement Bar
	Date									
	Goal									25 50 75 100
	Actual									
	Goal									25 50 75 100
	Actual									
	Goal									25 50 75 100
	Actual									
	Goal									25 50 75 100
	Actual									
	Goal									25 50 75 100
	Actual									

Daily/Weekly Tasks		Mon	Tue	Wed	Thur	Fri	Sat	Sun	Total	Achievement Bar
	Date									
	Goal									25 50 75 100
	Actual									
	Goal									25 50 75 100
	Actual									
	Goal									25 50 75 100
	Actual									
	Goal									25 50 75 100
	Actual									
	Goal									25 50 75 100
	Actual									

Daily/Weekly Tasks		Mon	Tue	Wed	Thur	Fri	Sat	Sun	Total	Achievement Bar
	Date									
	Goal									25 50 75 100
	Actual									
	Goal									25 50 75 100
	Actual									
	Goal									25 50 75 100
	Actual									
	Goal									25 50 75 100
	Actual									
	Goal									25 50 75 100
	Actual									

5-Minute Mindset
The

| | | Step 4: Design a Plan |
| Step 5: Implement a Plan |
Daily/Weekly Goal Tracker

Month_____

GOAL(S)

Daily/Weekly Tasks	Date	Mon	Tue	Wed	Thur	Fri	Sat	Sun	Total	Achievement Bar
	Goal									25 50 75 100
	Actual									
	Goal									25 50 75 100
	Actual									
	Goal									25 50 75 100
	Actual									
	Goal									25 50 75 100
	Actual									
	Goal									25 50 75 100
	Actual									

Daily/Weekly Tasks	Date	Mon	Tue	Wed	Thur	Fri	Sat	Sun	Total	Achievement Bar
	Goal									25 50 75 100
	Actual									
	Goal									25 50 75 100
	Actual									
	Goal									25 50 75 100
	Actual									
	Goal									25 50 75 100
	Actual									
	Goal									25 50 75 100
	Actual									

Daily/Weekly Tasks	Date	Mon	Tue	Wed	Thur	Fri	Sat	Sun	Total	Achievement Bar
	Goal									25 50 75 100
	Actual									
	Goal									25 50 75 100
	Actual									
	Goal									25 50 75 100
	Actual									
	Goal									25 50 75 100
	Actual									

5-Minute Mindset

Step 4: Design a Plan
Step 5: Implement a Plan
Daily/Weekly Goal Tracker

Month_____

GOAL(S)

Daily/Weekly Tasks	Date	Mon	Tue	Wed	Thur	Fri	Sat	Sun	Total	Achievement Bar
	Goal									25 50 75 100
	Actual									
	Goal									25 50 75 100
	Actual									
	Goal									25 50 75 100
	Actual									
	Goal									25 50 75 100
	Actual									
	Goal									25 50 75 100
	Actual									

Daily/Weekly Tasks	Date	Mon	Tue	Wed	Thur	Fri	Sat	Sun	Total	Achievement Bar
	Goal									25 50 75 100
	Actual									
	Goal									25 50 75 100
	Actual									
	Goal									25 50 75 100
	Actual									
	Goal									25 50 75 100
	Actual									
	Goal									25 50 75 100
	Actual									

Daily/Weekly Tasks	Date	Mon	Tue	Wed	Thur	Fri	Sat	Sun	Total	Achievement Bar
	Goal									25 50 75 100
	Actual									
	Goal									25 50 75 100
	Actual									
	Goal									25 50 75 100
	Actual									
	Goal									25 50 75 100
	Actual									
	Goal									25 50 75 100
	Actual									

5 The Minute Mindset

Step 4: Design a Plan
Step 5: Implement a Plan
Daily/Weekly Goal Tracker

Month_____

GOAL(S)

Daily/Weekly Tasks		Mon	Tue	Wed	Thur	Fri	Sat	Sun	Total	Achievement Bar
	Date									
	Goal									25 50 75 100
	Actual									
	Goal									25 50 75 100
	Actual									
	Goal									25 50 75 100
	Actual									
	Goal									25 50 75 100
	Actual									
	Goal									25 50 75 100
	Actual									

Daily/Weekly Tasks		Mon	Tue	Wed	Thur	Fri	Sat	Sun	Total	Achievement Bar
	Date									
	Goal									25 50 75 100
	Actual									
	Goal									25 50 75 100
	Actual									
	Goal									25 50 75 100
	Actual									
	Goal									25 50 75 100
	Actual									
	Goal									25 50 75 100
	Actual									

Daily/Weekly Tasks		Mon	Tue	Wed	Thur	Fri	Sat	Sun	Total	Achievement Bar
	Date									
	Goal									25 50 75 100
	Actual									
	Goal									25 50 75 100
	Actual									
	Goal									25 50 75 100
	Actual									
	Goal									25 50 75 100
	Actual									

The 5-Minute Mindset

Step 4: Design a Plan
Step 5: Implement a Plan
Daily/Weekly Goal Tracker

Month_____

GOAL(S)

Daily/Weekly Tasks		Mon	Tue	Wed	Thur	Fri	Sat	Sun	Total	Achievement Bar
	Date									
	Goal									25 50 75 100
	Actual									
	Goal									25 50 75 100
	Actual									
	Goal									25 50 75 100
	Actual									
	Goal									25 50 75 100
	Actual									
	Goal									25 50 75 100
	Actual									

Daily/Weekly Tasks		Mon	Tue	Wed	Thur	Fri	Sat	Sun	Total	Achievement Bar
	Date									
	Goal									25 50 75 100
	Actual									
	Goal									25 50 75 100
	Actual									
	Goal									25 50 75 100
	Actual									
	Goal									25 50 75 100
	Actual									
	Goal									25 50 75 100
	Actual									

Daily/Weekly Tasks		Mon	Tue	Wed	Thur	Fri	Sat	Sun	Total	Achievement Bar
	Date									
	Goal									25 50 75 100
	Actual									
	Goal									25 50 75 100
	Actual									
	Goal									25 50 75 100
	Actual									
	Goal									25 50 75 100
	Actual									
	Goal									25 50 75 100
	Actual									

5-Minute Mindset
The

Step 4: Design a Plan
Step 5: Implement a Plan
Daily/Weekly Goal Tracker   Month_____

GOAL(S)

Daily/Weekly Tasks		Mon	Tue	Wed	Thur	Fri	Sat	Sun	Total	Achievement Bar
	Date									
	Goal									25 50 75 100
	Actual									
	Goal									25 50 75 100
	Actual									
	Goal									25 50 75 100
	Actual									
	Goal									25 50 75 100
	Actual									
	Goal									25 50 75 100
	Actual									

Daily/Weekly Tasks		Mon	Tue	Wed	Thur	Fri	Sat	Sun	Total	Achievement Bar
	Date									
	Goal									25 50 75 100
	Actual									
	Goal									25 50 75 100
	Actual									
	Goal									25 50 75 100
	Actual									
	Goal									25 50 75 100
	Actual									
	Goal									25 50 75 100
	Actual									

Daily/Weekly Tasks		Mon	Tue	Wed	Thur	Fri	Sat	Sun	Total	Achievement Bar
	Date									
	Goal									25 50 75 100
	Actual									
	Goal									25 50 75 100
	Actual									
	Goal									25 50 75 100
	Actual									
	Goal									25 50 75 100
	Actual									
	Goal									25 50 75 100
	Actual									

The 5-Minute Mindset

Step 4: Design a Plan
Step 5: Implement a Plan
Daily/Weekly Goal Tracker

Month_____

GOAL(S)

Daily/Weekly Tasks		Mon	Tue	Wed	Thur	Fri	Sat	Sun	Total	Achievement Bar
	Date									
	Goal									25 50 75 100
	Actual									
	Goal									25 50 75 100
	Actual									
	Goal									25 50 75 100
	Actual									
	Goal									25 50 75 100
	Actual									
	Goal									25 50 75 100
	Actual									

Daily/Weekly Tasks		Mon	Tue	Wed	Thur	Fri	Sat	Sun	Total	Achievement Bar
	Date									
	Goal									25 50 75 100
	Actual									
	Goal									25 50 75 100
	Actual									
	Goal									25 50 75 100
	Actual									
	Goal									25 50 75 100
	Actual									
	Goal									25 50 75 100
	Actual									

Daily/Weekly Tasks		Mon	Tue	Wed	Thur	Fri	Sat	Sun	Total	Achievement Bar
	Date									
	Goal									25 50 75 100
	Actual									
	Goal									25 50 75 100
	Actual									
	Goal									25 50 75 100
	Actual									
	Goal									25 50 75 100
	Actual									
	Goal									25 50 75 100
	Actual									

The 5-Minute Mindset

Step 4: Design a Plan
Step 5: Implement a Plan

Month_____

Daily/Weekly Goal Tracker

GOAL(S)

Daily/Weekly Tasks		Mon	Tue	Wed	Thur	Fri	Sat	Sun	Total	Achievement Bar
	Date									
	Goal									25 50 75 100
	Actual									
	Goal									25 50 75 100
	Actual									
	Goal									25 50 75 100
	Actual									
	Goal									25 50 75 100
	Actual									
	Goal									25 50 75 100
	Actual									

Daily/Weekly Tasks		Mon	Tue	Wed	Thur	Fri	Sat	Sun	Total	Achievement Bar
	Date									
	Goal									25 50 75 100
	Actual									
	Goal									25 50 75 100
	Actual									
	Goal									25 50 75 100
	Actual									
	Goal									25 50 75 100
	Actual									
	Goal									25 50 75 100
	Actual									

Daily/Weekly Tasks		Mon	Tue	Wed	Thur	Fri	Sat	Sun	Total	Achievement Bar
	Date									
	Goal									25 50 75 100
	Actual									
	Goal									25 50 75 100
	Actual									
	Goal									25 50 75 100
	Actual									
	Goal									25 50 75 100
	Actual									

<table>
<tr><td colspan="3">The 5-Minute Mindset</td><td colspan="8">Step 4: Design a Plan
Step 5: Implement a Plan
Daily/Weekly Goal Tracker</td><td colspan="2">Month_____</td></tr>
</table>

GOAL(S)

Daily/Weekly Tasks		Mon	Tue	Wed	Thur	Fri	Sat	Sun	Total	Achievement Bar
	Date									
	Goal									25 50 75 100
	Actual									
	Goal									25 50 75 100
	Actual									
	Goal									25 50 75 100
	Actual									
	Goal									25 50 75 100
	Actual									
	Goal									25 50 75 100
	Actual									

Daily/Weekly Tasks		Mon	Tue	Wed	Thur	Fri	Sat	Sun	Total	Achievement Bar
	Date									
	Goal									25 50 75 100
	Actual									
	Goal									25 50 75 100
	Actual									
	Goal									25 50 75 100
	Actual									
	Goal									25 50 75 100
	Actual									
	Goal									25 50 75 100
	Actual									

Daily/Weekly Tasks		Mon	Tue	Wed	Thur	Fri	Sat	Sun	Total	Achievement Bar
	Date									
	Goal									25 50 75 100
	Actual									
	Goal									25 50 75 100
	Actual									
	Goal									25 50 75 100
	Actual									
	Goal									25 50 75 100
	Actual									
	Goal									25 50 75 100
	Actual									

5 The 5-Minute Mindset

Step 6: Provide Ongoing Motivation
Step 7: Interpret Results and Adjust Accordingly
Step 8: Celebrate Your Success
Step 9: Arrive at Your Destination

Date	Entries

The 5-Minute Mindset

Step 6: Provide Ongoing Motivation
Step 7: Interpret Results and Adjust Accordingly
Step 8: Celebrate Your Success
Step 9: Arrive at Your Destination

Date	Entries

5-Minute Mindset The

Step 6: Provide Ongoing Motivation
Step 7: Interpret Results and Adjust Accordingly
Step 8: Celebrate Your Success
Step 9: Arrive at Your Destination

Date	Entries

The 5-Minute Mindset

Step 6: Provide Ongoing Motivation
Step 7: Interpret Results and Adjust Accordingly
Step 8: Celebrate Your Success
Step 9: Arrive at Your Destination

Date	Entries

Acknowledgements

I'd like to thank the following people:

My wife and family for their encouragement and ideas.

My brother Rick, for helping develop and design the workbook.

Tonya Roberts, for her input and help in editing the book.

Travis Kelly for his artwork on the cover.

About the Author

Bob is a Real Estate Broker by profession. He has worked in the Real Estate industry since 1985.

Over the years he has trained hundreds of agents in the art of successful sales and marketing.

From 1988 to 2008 he served as president of Rocky Mountain Mortgage Inc., developing a very successful program that generated thousands of loans in over eight states.

What he learned over these years as a successful businessman certainly qualifies him as a man who understands the importance of having the right mindset in achieving success.

Now he is helping others achieve success through **"The 5-Minute Mindset for Success Workbook"** and other books.

Visit us at: www.The5-MinuteMindset.com

www.ingramcontent.com/pod-product-compliance
Lightning Source LLC
Chambersburg PA
CBHW081147270326

41930CB00014B/3068